Right-Brained Multiplication & Division

a Forget Memorization book

Effortless learning through images, stories, hands-on activities, and patterns

by Sarah Major

www.child1st.com

Right-Brained Multiplication & Division

To request more information regarding the copyright policy, contact:

Child1st Publications LLC

800-881-0912

info@child1st.com

For other teaching and learning resources designed for visual, tactile, kinesthetic and other right-brained
learners, visit www.child1st.com.

Other books and materials by this author:

Alphabet Tales
The Illustrated Book of Sounds & Their Spelling Patterns
The Easy-for-Me™ Books, sets A and B
The Easy-for-Me™ Reading Program
Kid-Friendly Math Series
Writing the Visual, Kinesthetic and Auditory Alphabet
SnapWords® sight word cards and SnapLetters™ stylized alphabet
I Can Sing from 1 to 10
SnapWords® Spelling Dictionary

ABOUT THIS BOOK

This book is for children who are strongly visual, who learn all at once through pictures, are drawn to patterns, rely on body motions, and who need to understand the process behind each math problem they solve. Child1st teaching and learning resources all follow the principle of conveying learning pieces using a variety of right-brain-friendly elements. We take learning tidbits that utilize symbols (numbers and letters) and abstractions, which are left-brained, and embed them in right-brained elements to beautifully integrate the left and right hemispheres in the brain.

RIGHT-BRAINED ELEMENTS:

1- We embed symbols in **VISUALS** so that the child can take a quick look, absorb the learning piece, and store it as an image to be retrieved intact later.

2- We use **PERSONIFICATION** which is a powerful element in teaching and learning. The use of personification makes for rapid learning because the very look and personality of the character conveys the substance of the learning. For example, Zeroman with his circular body, bouffant hair style, leer, and magic wand will be an unforgettable visual reminder that when a child multiplies or divides by zero, the magic wand will slash the air and the number will be transformed into a zero. POOSH! Instant learning!

3- We rely on **PATTERN DISCOVERY** as a way of making numbers come alive and as a means of conveying the amazing relationships between numbers. What results is number sense. Because the brain is a pattern seeking organ, it is drawn to material that follows patterns. It is my desire that through this teaching resource, many children who are overwhelmed or daunted by math might come to truly be fascinated by it instead.

4- We use **STORY** to contain the meaning of what we are teaching in math. Stories, like visuals, make learning unforgettable. They explain the "why" behind math concepts and tie everything together, creating a vehicle for meaning and for recall.

5- We use **BODY MOTION**—both gesture and whole body movement. Some of the movement includes clapping and chanting, while some is acting out the story of the individual table. Again, body movement is a powerful agent for learning and remembering. For many people, body motion makes recall effortless if the learning piece is directly tied to a unique motion.

6- We employ **VISUALIZATION**—a powerful tool for right-brain-dominant learners. If they are given time to transfer the image on the paper in front of them to their brains (prompt them to close their eyes and SEE it in their mind's eye), they will be able to retrieve that image later. If the image contains learning concepts, this is how they will remember what you want them to learn. So in this book, each time a visual is introduced, prompt the student(s) to "see" the image in their mind, eyes closed.

Multiplication and Division TEACHING CARDS

We've created full color teaching cards for classroom display to accompany this book. The cards each have a character such as Zeroman or a visual of a problem such as 5 x 9 = 45. While all the visuals are included in this book, if you desire to display the stylized facts on a wall, bulletin board or in a pocket chart, visit www.child1st.com and search for Multiplication and Division Teaching Cards. Use code MDCARDS for 10% off your order. Color, 8.5" x 5.5".

HOW TOs

1- Scan the chart on page 5, which shows the total number of facts to be learned. This chart is an important piece that will allow your student(s) to track their own progress. Supply each child with a chart of their own so they can color each square as they master facts. It is important for the child(ren) to both see how many concepts they need to learn and to monitor their own progress.

2- Familiarize yourself with the various characters and stories in the book before beginning to teach any of it. The text in the book is directed to the student(s) rather than the teacher. This will make it simple for the teacher or parent to teach the content, but do be sure that you prepare ahead of time so you're not just reading the content to the child(ren).

3- If you are teaching one child or a small group, share the illustrations in the book as you go through the lesson. Each chapter includes full-sized illustrations that will enhance your child(ren)'s visual memory of the tables. Allow them time to really study the image and to visually imprint it on their minds.

4- Let the child(ren) absorb at their own pace rather than rushing them into drill and memorization. Memorization of facts might seem to be the most direct route to learning multiplication and division, but it is least effective in the long run.

5- Photocopy the practice problems from Appendix A before starting each chapter. The problem section numbers are included in each chapter for reference. It is important to stop and practice often as you progress through the chapter. The hands-on time will make learning stick.

6- Teach the tables in the order presented in this book, rather than going in numerical order. The sequence of lessons was designed to be as kid-friendly as possible. We have grouped tables together that are closely related such as zero and 10s, and 1s and 11s, and we have the 12s following closely behind 2s as their answers are very similar.

7- Allow plenty of time to practice; encourage the child(ren) to monitor their own fluency with the facts and teach them to ask for more practice problems if they are not completely sure they know their facts. Allow time for the child(ren) to retell stories, to draw their own pictures for the problems, and to share what they are learning with another child or adult. All this will deepen their learning and enhance recall.

8- More than one way to learn the facts is presented in each chapter. Follow each child's lead in finding the method that works the best for him/her. A valuable practice while going through this book is to lead your child(ren) into a better understanding of how they most efficiently learn and remember. I always ask children "How did you remember that?" or "How can you remember that?" Once children understand that they have more than one good way to learn something, they will pay attention to what works for them.

9- Appendix B contains an answer key to save you time as you check your child(ren)'s work.

SYMBOLS USED IN THIS BOOK

 The book symbol identifies stories about times tables and also identifies story problems.

 The hand symbol identifies hands-on activities throughout the chapters.

 The pencil cup draws attention to practice problems and where they are found in Appendix A.

 The division symbol accompanies explanation of division procedures in each chapter.

 The multiplication symbol accompanies explanation of multiplication procedures.

This chart shows the multiplication and division facts your child(ren) need to learn. The brown bar at the top shows the order in which we will learn the tables. As the child learns one set of facts, she should color in those boxes so she can chart her progress. 10s are done for you.

Because many facts overlap (such as 2 x 5 and 5 x 2) we have not included the bottom half of the chart. Your child will be excited to see his progress!

Multiplication & Division Facts   Name_____

Start date:		#3	#7	#8	#5	#9	#10	#11	#6	#1	#2	#4
	1x	2x	3x	4x	5x	6x	7x	8x	9x	10x	11x	12x
1≈	1	2	3	4	5	6	7	8	9	10	11	12
2≈		4	6	8	10	12	14	16	18	20	22	24
3≈			9	12	15	18	21	24	27	30	33	36
4≈				16	20	24	28	32	36	40	44	48
5≈					25	30	35	40	45	50	55	60
6≈						36	42	48	54	60	66	72
7≈							49	56	63	70	77	84
8≈								64	72	80	88	96
9≈									81	90	99	108
10≈										100	110	120
11≈											121	132
12≈												144

DAILY PROCEDURE:

- Copy necessary practice sheets.

- Display appropriate teaching card if you are teaching more than one child (see info on the bottom of page 3).

- Share with the child(ren) the story that explains the chapter's character. **Stories are in italics.** *Story problems are blue.*

- Emphasize the visuals as a means of remembering how to solve each times table.

- Allow for plenty of practice. If you need more problem sheets than what is provided in Appendix A, any multiplication and division practice sheets will work to supply ample practice. Be sure to do the hands-on activities.

- Teach multiplication and division together as mirror processes—trios of numbers allow for both functions. For example, 3 x 5 = 15, 5 x 3 = 15, 15 ÷ 3 = 5, and 15 ÷ 5 = 3. Make sure the child(ren) understand that the two small numbers in each trio can switch places with each other, but the large number in each trio stays put. You could not, for example, say 15 ÷ 3 = 5 and 3 ÷ 15 = 5. The 15 stays put and the small numbers, 3 and 5, can switch places.

TABLE OF CONTENTS & LEARNING FOCUS FOR EACH CHAPTER

Each chapter is different from the others. Below each chapter title, the focus provided will be the pathway to the brain or the primary elements that will help the student(s) learn and recall the multiplication and division facts. Emphasize these as you go through the lesson. After each lesson, take time to ask the student(s) which element was most effective in helping them learn and remember their facts.

ZEROMAN & MR. 10 STIR THINGS UP

ZEROMAN WAVES HIS WAND:

Zeroman is a really fun guy. His name means "none," but he can make a 10 out of a 1 or a 50 out of a 5. Zeroman has a magic wand and can turn numbers into zeros with one big POOOSH of his magic wand!

If you see 0 x 2 it means "no 2s." Your 2s just vanished. And if you see 2 x 0 it means you have 2 zeros. You just have zeros which means you have nothing.

Look at this chart! 0 x any number is....Zeroman!

Chart for 0x				
0 x 1 = 0	0 x 2 = 0	0 x 3 = 0	0 x 4 = 0	0 x 5 = 0
0 x 6 = 0	0 x 7 = 0	0 x 8 = 0	0 x 9 = 0	0 x 10 = 0
0 x 11 = 0	0 x 12 = 0			

STORY 1: You, Jon, and Mary are at the store. Mary asks, "How many dimes do you have?" You say, "I have zero dimes." Jon answers, "I have 2 dimes." When you say "I have zero dimes" you are telling Mary you have no dimes at all.

STORY 2: Tom, Jon, and Mary are at the track field. The track is two miles long. Jon ran around the track five times. Mary ran around the track six times. Tom held the watch and timed their run (in other words, Tom just stood there and didn't run at all).

Let's make story 2 into three problems:

Jon ran 5 times around the 2 mile track for a total of 10 miles.   So 5 x 2 = 10.
Mary ran 6 times around the 2 mile track for a total of 12 miles.   So 6 x 2 = 12.
Tom ran 0 times around the 2 mile track for a total of 0 miles.   So 0 x 2 = 0.

HANDS-ON:
Take a scrap sheet of paper.
Write these numbers, one on each line: 5; 71; 125; 26; 86; 42; 12,356; 456; 24; 19.
Now go back and multiply each one by 0. Also do the tactile and kinesthetic activities on page 14 either now or after doing page 9.

PRACTICE PROBLEMS:
Use sheet 1.1 from page 92.

RULE: 0 x any number = 0

STORY 3: Mr. Ray was making lunches for his three kids. He gave each of them 5 grapes, 1 milk and 0 candy. This is what he gave them:

Grapes x 5
Milk x 1
Candy x 0

Let's make story 3 into problems:

3 kids x 5 grapes = 15 grapes in all
3 kids x 1 milk = 3 milks in all
3 kids x 0 candy = 0 candy in all

15 grapes shared by 3 kids = 5 grapes each
3 milks shared by 3 kids = 1 milk each
0 candy shared by 3 kids = 0 candy each

grapes   milk   candy

HANDS-ON:

Pretend you are making lunch for 3 kids. Decide what you will give them and draw a picture of the food or use plastic objects to represent parts of the lunches. Next, write problems for the lunches like we did in the example at the top of the page. Use the following for examples of multiplication and division:

MULTIPLICATION:

3 kids x _____ (# of items) = _____ in all.

DIVISION:

_____(# of items) shared between 3 kids = _____ each.

PRACTICE PROBLEMS:
Use sheet 1.2 from page 92.

RULE: 0 ÷ any number = 0

Mr. 10 is a guy who loves colored rings. He has collected rings in many colors. He loves to share, so whenever anyone comes by, he quickly tosses them a ring. Look what happened when these numbers came into his room!

When you multiply by 10, you can be Mr. 10 tossing brightly colored rings to any number you are multiplying by.

10 x 2 = 2 and a ring, or 20

10 x 4 = 4 and a ring, or 40

10 x 9 = 9 and a ring, or 90

10 x 5 = 5 and a ring, or 50

10 x 512 = 512 and a ring, or 5120

Check out the chart for 10x and look for patterns. What do you see?

Chart for 10x				
10 x 1 = 10	10 x 2 = 20	10 x 3 = 30	10 x 4 = 40	10 x 5 = 50
10 x 6 = 60	10 x 7 = 70	10 x 8 = 80	10 x 9 = 90	10 x 10 = 100
10 x 11 = 110	10 x 12 = 120			

HANDS-ON:
Take a piece of scratch paper. Write 10 numbers on the paper—any numbers you want. Now exchange papers with a friend. Each of you will multiply your ten numbers by 10. Talk about your answers when you are finished. Wasn't that easy?

PRACTICE PROBLEMS:
Use sheet 1.3 from page 93.

RULE: 10 x any number = that number with a 0 after it

Division with 10s is really fun! Start with a big number that ends in a zero, say 510; if you divide it by 10, you just take the zero off the end! When you are practicing, just put your thumb over the zero and you will see the answer.

$$40 \div 10 = 4 \qquad 230 \div 10 = 23 \qquad 150 \div 10 = 15$$

Show the child(ren) that 5 x 10 looks like this:	You add all the zeros to get a zero and then all the 1's in the tens place to get 5 tens or 50.
10 10 10 10 10 ___ 50	The shortcut is just to add a zero to the end of any number. When dividing by 10, the question is how many 10s are in 50 and the answer is simply "Look at the 10s place: there are **5** tens in **50**."

HANDS-ON:

Take a piece of scratch paper. Write 10 numbers on the paper—any numbers you want that end in a zero (every number must end in a zero in order to divide evenly by 10). Now exchange papers with a friend. Each of you will divide your numbers by 10. Talk about your answers when you are finished. Also do the activities for the 10s on page 14.

PRACTICE PROBLEMS:

Use sheet 1.4 from page 93.

RULE: any number ÷ 10 = that number without the 0 on the end

Guy Hundred:

Guy Hundred is Mr. 10's grandfather. They look a lot alike and both like to throw colored rings, but Guy Hundred has two zeros instead of just one and throws 2 rings instead of 1.

To multiply by 100, just think of Guy Hundred tossing 2 rings to each number being multiplied.

So, 100 x 5 = 500

To divide by 100, just take back the colored rings.

So, 500 ÷ 100 = 5

Show the child(ren) that 3 x 100 looks like this:	100 100 100 ___ 300

You add all the zeros straight down and then all the 1's in the hundreds place to get 3 hundreds, or 300. The shortcut is just to add 2 zeros to the end of any number.

In dividing by 100, the question is how many 100s are in 300, and the answer is simply "There are 3 hundreds in 300."

HANDS-ON:
Take a piece of scratch paper. In one column, write 10 numbers. These will be multiplied by 100. In the second column, write 10 numbers that end in two 0s. These will be divided by 100. Exchange papers with a friend and solve. Talk about your answers when you are finished.

PRACTICE PROBLEMS:
Use sheets 1.5 and 1.6 from page 94.

> ## RULE: 100 x any number = that number and 00 after it

> ## RULE: any number ÷ 100 = that number without the 00

JUST SUPPOSE...

Do you suppose that the zero rules would work for any number of zeros?

YES it does! Let's try it (write problems on scratch paper or whiteboard):

$$1{,}000 \times 2 = 2{,}000 \qquad\qquad 1{,}000 \times 76 = 76{,}000$$

$$2{,}000 \div 1{,}000 = 2 \qquad\qquad 76{,}000 \div 1{,}000 = 76$$

IT'S YOUR TURN TO MAKE SOME PROBLEMS:
Demonstrate the following by writing on a whiteboard or scrap of paper. Work the problems out together. First write any numbers you want in the first column. Solve for 1000 x the numbers you wrote. Notice that if you take the answers to the first set of problems and write them into the third column, once you divide by 1000, your 1st and 4th columns should be exactly alike. One is done for you.

76	x 1,000 =	76,000		76,000	÷ 1,000 =	76
_____	x 1,000 =	_____		_____	÷ 1,000 =	_____
_____	x 1,000 =	_____		_____	÷ 1,000 =	_____
_____	x 1,000 =	_____		_____	÷ 1,000 =	_____

PRACTICE PROBLEMS:
Use sheet 1.7 from page 95.

Tactile and kinesthetic activities for 0s

IN THE CLASSROOM:

Choose a child to be Zeroman. He will have a magic wand and wear a card on his chest that has a big zero on it. The other children will have cards with numbers from 1–9 on them.

ADDITION & SUBTRACTION: In this type of problem, you are adding nothing and subtracting nothing. Children will show that adding # (number) + 0 will result in the child with the # jumping in front of Zeroman to become the answer (Ex: 4 + 0 = 4). For subtraction: When acting out the problem 4 - 0, the four will once again jump in front of Zeroman to become the answer.

MULTIPLICATION & DIVISION: In this type of problem you have zero times a # and sharing a # among zero people. Zeroman will wave his wand to make #s into 0s. So you can have one child at a time become a multiplication or division problem with the Zeroman. If you display 8 x 0 =, Zeroman will wave his magic wand and POOF, Zeroman will jump in front of the child with the number.

AT HOME:

ADDITION & SUBTRACTION: Your child can use magnetic numbers to make the addition and subtraction problems. If he displays 4 + 0, prompt him to grab the 4 from the beginning of the problem and make it the answer. The same goes for 4 - 0. He will grab the 4 from the problem and make it the answer.

MULTIPLICATION AND DIVISION: Have your child use a pencil or a wand of her own design to "POOF" the numbers away, leaving just Zeroman.

Tactile and kinesthetic activities for 10s

IN THE CLASSROOM:

Choose a child to be Mr. 10. He will have colored rings (made from construction paper, for example) and wear a card on his chest that has a big 10 on it. Other children will wear cards with numbers from 1–9 on them.

MULTIPLICATION: Children will show that multiplying by 10 means they will receive a colored ring from Mr. 10 and hold it up beside them.

DIVISION: Have the children show that dividing by 10 means he will take back his colored rings. If you write the problems on the whiteboard or chart paper while they are acting out the problems, it will be easier for them to relate the symbols and the written version of the problem to the movements they are making with their bodies.

AT HOME:

Your child can use magnetic numbers or numbers cut from construction paper. To solve any problem that is multiplied by 10, the child will just put a colored 0 after the number. For example, if he is solving 10 x 6, he will add a colored ring to the 6 to make the answer.

For division, (say 60 ÷ 10) he will simply remove the 0 from the 60 to arrive at the answer.

Agent 1

MEET AGENT 1 & DOUBLE AGENT 11

LOVELY AGENT 1:

Agent 1 is an agent, but she's also a kind and sweet person. She likes people and sweetly points at them saying, "Just be yourself, dahling!"

If 55 asks, "How many is you times me?" for example, Agent 1 points and says, "Just be yourself!"

Along comes 4,567. He asks, "How many is you times me?" Agent 1 says, "Just be yourself." What do you think the answer will be? Why, 4,567, of course! 1 x any number at all will be itself!

> ### RULE: any number x 1 or ÷ 1 = that number

PRACTICE PROBLEMS:
Use sheets 2.1 and 2.2 from page 96.

HANDS-ON:
Do activities for Agent 1 on page 22.

AGENT OLIVER BECOMES DOUBLE AGENT 11:

Chart for 11x				
11 x 1 = 11	11 x 2 = 22	11 x 3 = 33	11 x 4 = 44	11 x 5 = 55
11 x 6 = 66	11 x 7 = 77	11 x 8 = 88	11 x 9 = 99	11 x 10 = 110
11 x 11 = 121	11 x 12 = 132			

Notice in the 11x chart that 1 problem is blue. This is because you already know that 11 x 10 is 110. Take some time to find patterns in this chart. Talk about what you see.

Here is the scoop about the 11s chart:
Agent 1's friend Oliver studied hard and trained to become a Double Agent. He got the name Double Agent 11 from standing under streetlights at night and casting a shadow.

Double Agent 11 is too cool. He's smart, quick, and always gets the job done. Double Agent 11 hired a staff of great double agents that work for him, which shows he's smart and quick, and is why he always gets the job done!

Double Agent 11...

...has a shadow:

2 x 11 = #2 guy,
Double Agent 22

3 x 11 = #3 guy,
Double Agent 33

4 x 11 = #4 guy,
Double Agent 44

5 x 11 = #5 guy,
Double Agent 55

6 x 11 = #6 guy,
Double Agent 66

7 x 11 = #7 guy,
Double Agent 77

8 x 11 = #8 guy,
Double Agent 88

9 x 11 = #9 guy,
Double Agent 99

10 x 11 = #10 guy,
Double Agent 110

11 x 11 = #11 guy,
Double Agent 121

12 x 11 = #12 guy,
Double Agent 132

I think working with Double Agent 11 will make your work into play! If you multiply 11 x any number from 1–9, you just turn the number into a double agent, and you're done! For example:

11 x 6 = 66   You can see that 6 suddenly acquired a shadow (a double).

For any double number from 11 up to 99, when you divide by 11, all you do is hide the shadow:

55 ÷ 11 = 5   **99 ÷ 11 = 9**   **77 ÷ 11 = 7**

HANDS-ON:
Take a piece of scratch paper. In one column, write numbers from 1–9 out of order. Multiply these by 11. In the second column, write double numbers from 11–99 out of order and divide by 11.

PRACTICE PROBLEMS:
Use sheets 2.3 and 2.4 from page 97.

RULE: 11 x any number 1–9 = two of that number

RULE: double numbers 11–99 ÷ 11 = just one of the digits

---

11 X MULTI-DIGIT NUMBERS:

When you multiply 11 x a double digit number, the solution is really fun!
Look at 11 x 10, 11 x 11, and 11 x 12 (refer to visuals on page 19):

11 x 10 = 110 (Write the 10 spread apart like this: 1_0. Then add the two numbers and put the sum in the middle: 1 + 0 = 1. The 1 goes in the middle: 110).

11 x 11 = 121 (Write the 11 spread apart like this: 1_1. Then add the two numbers and put the sum in the middle: 1 + 1 = 2. The 2 goes in the middle: 121).

11 x 12 = 132 (Write the 12 spread apart like this: 1_2. Then add the two numbers and put the sum in the middle: 1 + 2 = 3. The 3 goes in the middle: 132).

HANDS-ON:
Take a piece of scratch paper. Make a column of these numbers: 13, 16, 14, 21, 45, 34, 52, 61. Multiply these numbers by 11. I bet you can also do them in your head! Say a number. Close your eyes until you can see it in your head. Then add the digits and put their sum in the middle.

PRACTICE PROBLEMS:
Use sheet 2.5 from page 98.

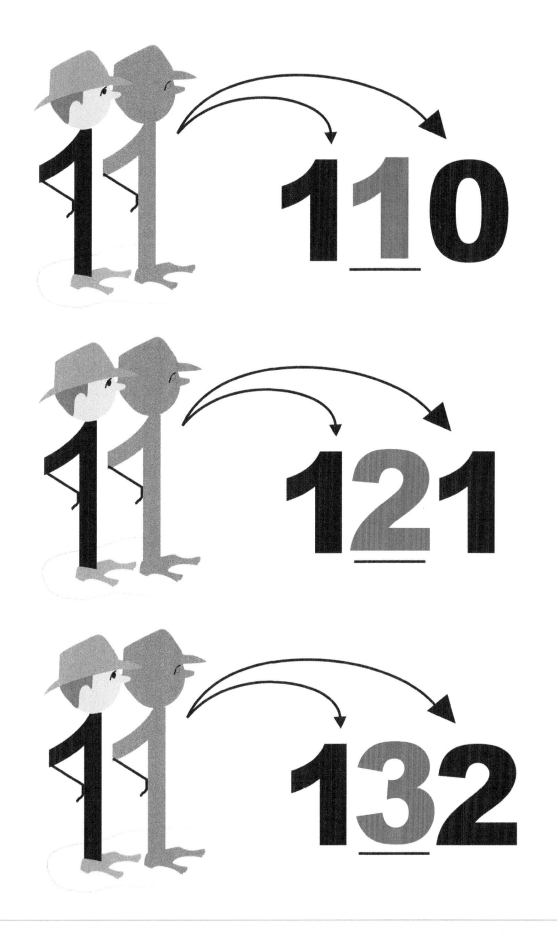

RULE: 11 x a double digit # = sum of the #s put between them

USE THE "WALL AND LINE" METHOD:

Let's solve 11 x 125 using the regular way. I call it the "wall and line" method.

Because
- 1 x any number is that same number
                    and
- 10 x a number is that same number with a zero after it,

multiplying by 11 means "1 of the number and 10 of the number."

In other words, if you remember that 11 means one 10 and one 1, you can write the problem out like this:

1 x 125 ———   **125**
10 x 125 ——— **+1250**
                ————————
Just be sure the   **1375**
right side of the

numbers are lined up by the wall, and then add the columns straight down.

USE A SHORTCUT:

We're going to solve 11 x 125 another way that requires less writing:

1- Write 125 like this: **12___5** (move the last number over to leave a space like you did on page 18).

2- Now add the numbers 12 + 5. The answer is **17**.

3- Write the **17** over the **12___5** so that the 7 drops into the space and the 1 is over the 2.

This is what you will have: 1
                                  1275
                                 ————
Now add straight down: 1375   So the answer to 11 x 125 is 1375.

HANDS-ON:
Take a piece of scratch paper. Make a column of these numbers, skipping 2 or 3 lines to give yourself enough room: 342, 231, 412, 154, 623. Now draw a line and a wall for each problem. Multiply by 1 first, then by 10, lining the numbers up so they are right next to the wall. Try the same problems using the shortcut. Which way do you like best?

PRACTICE PROBLEMS:
Use sheet 2.6 from page 98. Solve the problems using the method you like better—wall and line or shortcut.

To divide any DOUBLE NUMBER from 11 up to 99 by 11, all you do is hide the shadow:

$$55 \div 11 = 5\cancel{5} \qquad 99 \div 11 = 9\cancel{9} \qquad 77 \div 11 = 7\cancel{7}$$

That is super easy, right?

For THREE-DIGIT numbers, just get rid of the middle number:

11 x 10 = 110	110 ÷ 11 = 1$\cancel{1}$0 or 10
11 x 11 = 121	121 ÷ 11 = 1$\cancel{2}$1 or 11
11 x 12 = 132	132 ÷ 11 = 1$\cancel{3}$2 or 12
11 x 13 = 143	143 ÷ 11 = 1$\cancel{4}$3 or 13
11 x 14 = 154	154 ÷ 11 = 1$\cancel{5}$4 or 14

NOTE TO TEACHER:

The color-coding in the example problems above will be important for your student(s) to note. With repeated views of these examples, what will happen when your student sees regular problems that are not color-coded is that the numbers that are on the outside (red in these examples) will visually stand out to him. This is one of the amazing things about visual learners. So in the practice problems, when he sees 154 ÷ 11, his mind's eye will see the 14 in the 154. A pattern that will also emerge is that he will begin to notice numbers which have the sum of first and third digits in the middle (Ex: 121, 253, 154, 165, etc.). This will trigger the child to know he's doing a ÷11 problem.

HANDS-ON:

Take a piece of scratch paper. Make a column of these numbers: 15, 16, 17, 18. Multiply these by 11 using our trick. Put their answers in the second column and reverse the process, dividing them by 11—by just getting rid of the middle number. Check yourself using a calculator if you would like to.

PRACTICE PROBLEMS:

Use sheet 2.7 from page 99.

RULE: any double number from 11–99 ÷ 11, just hide the shadow

---

RULE: to divide a 3-digit number by 11, erase the middle digit

Tactile and kinesthetic activities for 1s

IN THE CLASSROOM:

MULTIPLICATION & DIVISION: Choose a child to be Agent 1. She will wear a big card with a 1 on it, and she could use a pointing stick. The other children will have cards with numbers from 1–9 on them. Have Agent 1 practice saying, "Just be yourself." The other children can arrange themselves in a row and make any number they want. The teacher should record the problems they make on the whiteboard.

Also, give each child several counters. Say, "1 x 6. Make that with your counters." The children will make 1 pile of 6 counters. For division say, "6 ÷ 1. There are 6 cookies to divide by one child. Show that with your counters." The children will pile up 6 counters for 1 child.

AT HOME:

MULTIPLICATION & DIVISION: Your child can use magnetic numbers or numbers cut from construction paper and create problems for himself. Have him arrange numbers on the table or fridge door and pretend to be Agent 1 who pronounces "Just be yourself." Alternately, he may draw a colorful poster, making problems which are solved by the pointing Agent 1. Also do the activity with counters just above.

Tactile and kinesthetic activities for 11s

IN THE CLASSROOM:

MULTIPLICATION: Choose 2 children to be Double Agent 11. The other children will have cards with numbers from 1–9 on them, at least two children for each number. First, the teacher will write a problem on the board and the children will act it out. For example, for the problem 9 x 11, one of the children wearing the number 9 would come forward along with the children acting out Double Agent 11. Then, the child wearing the number 9 and the second child wearing number 9 would move to the end of the problem to show the answer, 99. Next, the teacher will write a 2-digit problem on the board and the children will act that out. For example, when acting out 11 x 12, the children being Double Agent 11 would come forward along with a child wearing the number 1 and a child wearing the number 2. To form the answer, the 2 children wearing a 1 and a 2 would move to end of the problem and spread apart. The teacher should let all the children figure out which number (3) should come stand in between them to form the 3-digit answer. (Reminder: just add up the 2 numbers to get the middle number.)

DIVISION: Dividing by 11 will be just the opposite. Children will start with a two digit number such as 55 and when approached by Agent 11, the shadow will melt away and the answer will be the single digit 5.

AT HOME:

Your child can use magnetic or cut-out numbers.

MULTIPLICATION: To solve any problem that is multiplied by 11, the child will just add another identical number. For example, if she is solving 11 x 5, she will find two 5s to make her answer. For bigger numbers, have her pull the final digit to the right to leave a space in which she will insert the missing number (ex: 11 x 12 = 1__2, then add 1+2 and put the 3 in the space.)

DIVISION: To divide 55 ÷ 11, she will simply remove the shadow 5 from the 55 to arrive at the answer.

PRACTICE PROBLEMS:
Use sheet 2.8 from page 100.

MISS 2 SEES DOUBLE

Miss 2 put on her red dress one day and went for a walk. She always looked for pairs of things when she walked, and today she was hoping she'd find a lot of pairs!

I see a double!

Chart for 2x				
2 x 1 = 2	2 x 2 = 4	2 x 3 = 6	2 x 4 = 8	2 x 5 = 10
2 x 6 = 12	2 x 7 = 14	2 x 8 = 16	2 x 9 = 18	2 x 10 = 20
2 x 11 = 22	2 x 12 = 24			

Notice in this chart that three of the boxes are colored blue. This is because these are problems you already know. The purple box is a problem we will learn in another chapter. (Of course if you can learn it now, that's super!) Notice the number patterns in each column of answers.

23

Right away, Miss 2 saw two workers in hard hats building a purple boat with gold rivets to hold it together. A red flag fluttered in the breeze at the very top. Close your eyes and see the boat with the two workers on it. "Two 2s make a 4."

2 × 2 = 4

24

As she left the city, Miss 2 saw two mice living in a two-story house with a stick roof. Smoke curled from the chimney. The mice each had 3 pieces of cheese to eat. "They must eat a LOT of cheese," Miss 2 thought to herself. "They are the hugest mice I've ever seen! Why, each of them is as big as three mice! I will have to call each of them 'Triple Mouse.'"

Close your eyes and see the large house shaped like a 6 with straw for a roof, and then see the cheese. How many pieces are there, and where are they on the house? Finally, see the Triple Mice. Why did Miss 2 call them that?

2 × 3 =

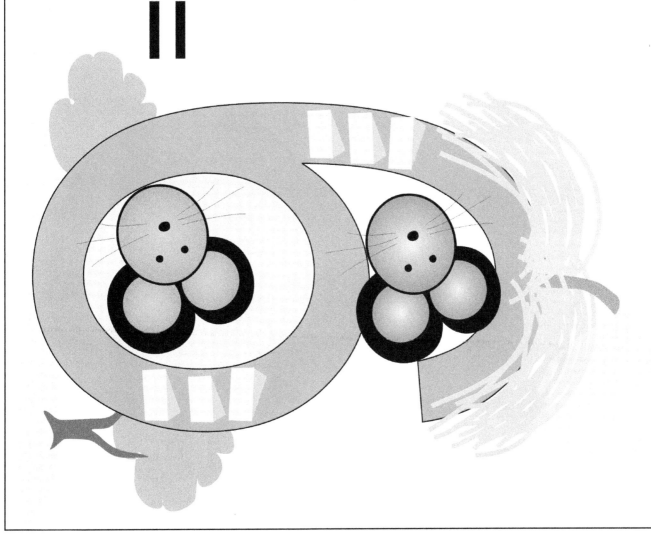

25

Soon Miss 2 came to the edge of a small town where she saw two boats floating in twin lakes with cattails growing along the edges. 8 yellow ducks sunned themselves by the lakes.

Remember the first pair Miss 2 saw? It was two workers making a boat. Don't these boats look like that one? Study the picture and notice the ducks sitting in 2s by the lakes. Now close your eyes and see this picture in your head. Describe what you see.

A little further down the path, Miss 2 spied two men walking in a park filled with green grass and flower beds. A streetlight shone brightly by the path.

Study the picture. The 10 is made of a lightpost and an oval park. See the men walking around the track. Now close your eyes and see the picture in your head. Do you see the two flower patches? How many flowers are in each patch?

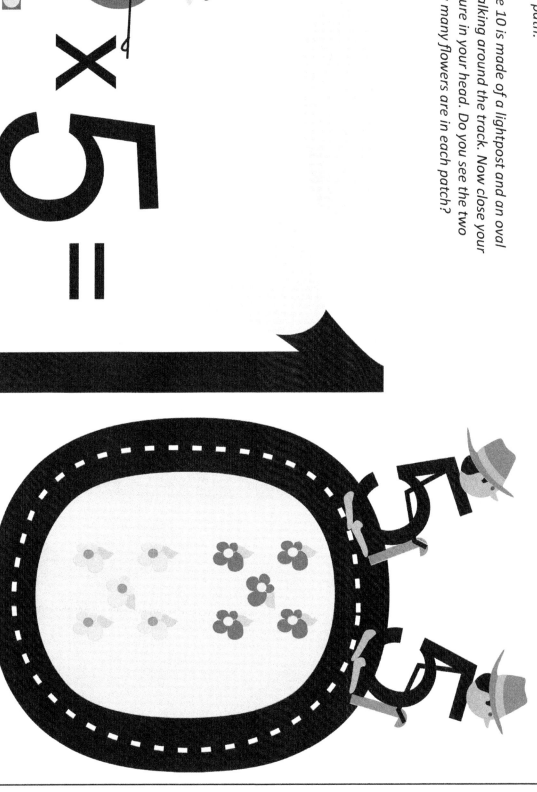

Miss 2 passed through an open gate where the largest chicken she had ever seen stood guard over two nests on a shelf. Miss 2 waved but did not come closer. She admired the hen's beautiful feathers, though.

Study the picture. Notice that the 1 in the 12 is a bench that holds two nests. Each nest has six eggs. Now close your eyes and describe all you can see. How many tail feathers does the huge hen have?

2 × 6 = 12

After a while, Miss 2 saw a tall house built from bent wood and painted a soft brown. There was a table and chair and a very bright light hanging from the ceiling. Miss 2 thought she might like to live there!

When you study this picture, can you see where two 7s are in the posts of the house? Notice the patterns of dots on each post. How many are there? Now with your eyes closed, describe all you can see in this picture.

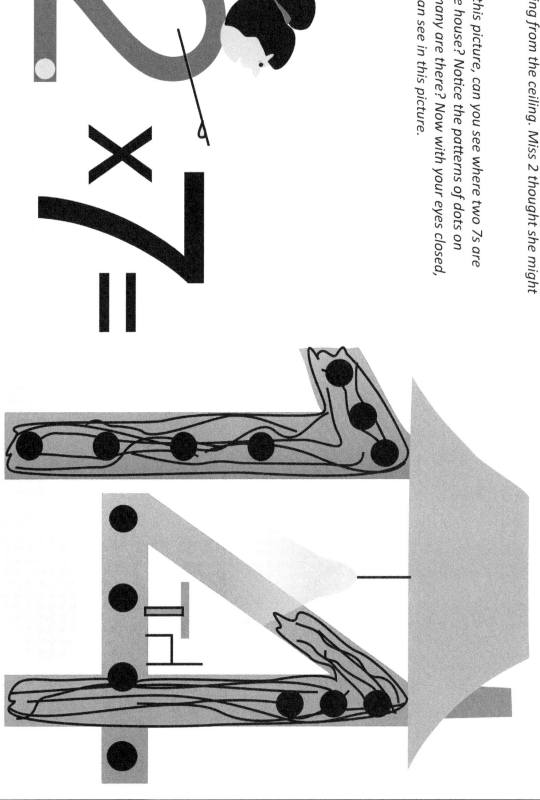

29

Miss 2 was getting pretty tired by this time, but she kept on going. When she saw two spiders on their web, however, she forgot about being tired and ran away very quickly!

Study this picture. What was the 6 last time you saw it? A nest, right? This time the 6 is a huge spiderweb by a tall post! Close your eyes and describe the web and the spiders. How many legs do the spiders have?

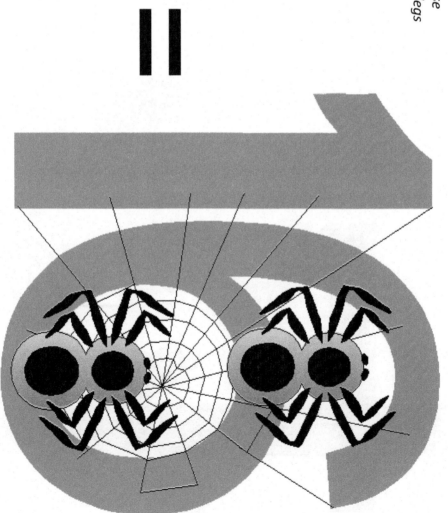

30

Miss 2 circled another pair of ponds but this time instead of boats, she saw two boys holding big red helium balloons. Miss 2 hoped the balloons didn't pick the boys up and drift off with them! It surely was beautiful in the country, but Miss 2 was ready to go home.

Study the picture. How many stepping stones are by each lake? Does the 1 in the 18 look like it might be a runway for small planes? How fun to land there and be able to walk around those lakes! Close your eyes and see this in your mind.

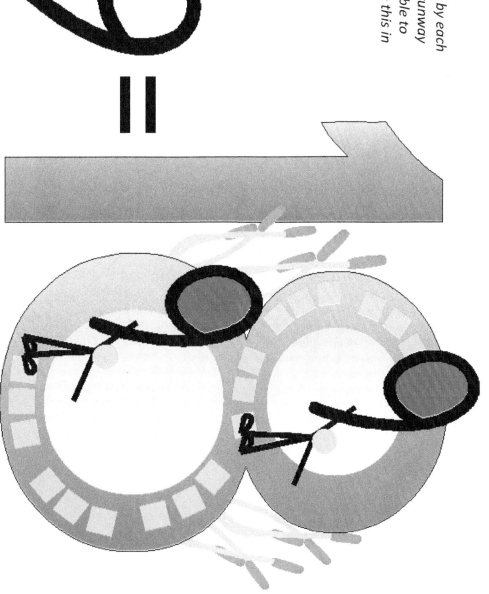

2 × 9 = 18

When Miss 2 got home, she fell asleep in her chair and dreamed about all the pairs she'd found on her walk.

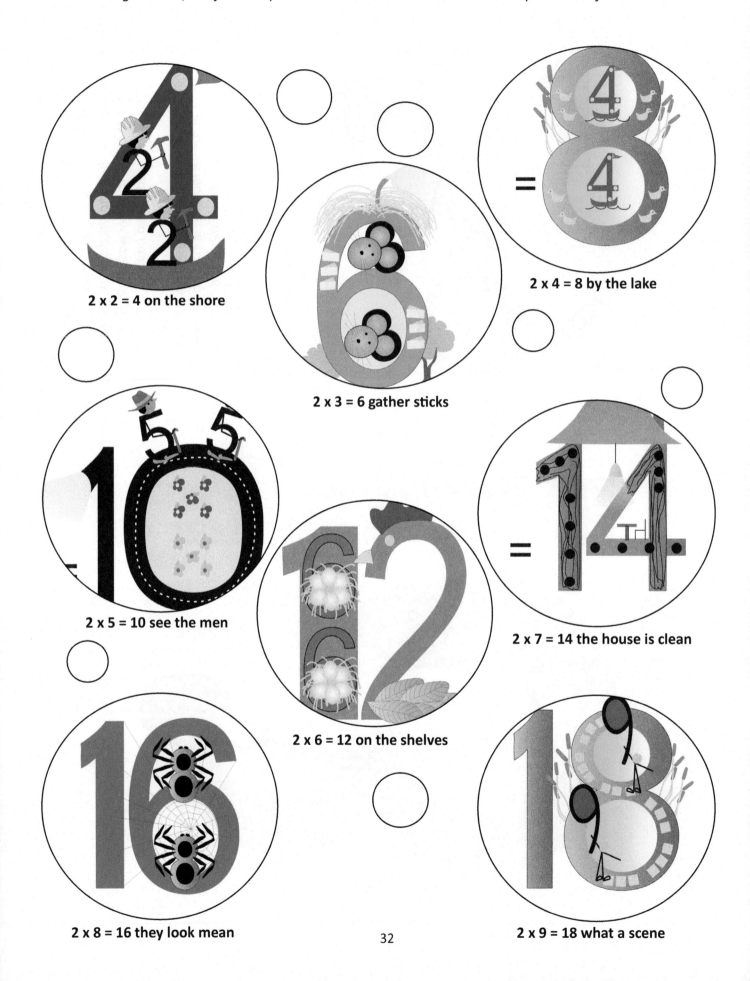

2 x 2 = 4 on the shore

2 x 3 = 6 gather sticks

2 x 4 = 8 by the lake

2 x 5 = 10 see the men

2 x 6 = 12 on the shelves

2 x 7 = 14 the house is clean

2 x 8 = 16 they look mean

2 x 9 = 18 what a scene

PRACTICE PROBLEMS:
Use sheets 3.1 and 3.2 from page 101.

Tactile and kinesthetic activities for learning 2s

IN THE CLASSROOM:

Choose a child to be Miss 2. Divide the rest of the class into the various groups of characters Miss 2 encountered on her walk. Each of the groups can prepare their props if desired (boat, house, lake, spiderweb, etc). Have Miss 2 walk around the classroom saying what she sees at each station.

Alternately, the children might enjoy each making a booklet in which they draw and illustrate the 2s facts. They can make up their own rhythmical wording for the problems (Ex: 2 x 4= 8 by the lake). Encourage them to share with the class their own best way of remembering, whether it be movement, drawings, jingles they say, or practice verbally answering from flashcards.

AT HOME:

Your child can make a book of the facts and write a simple story line for it. Or you could give her big cutouts of the numbers, have her glue them into place, one problem per page, and have her embellish the numbers to show the scenes in the story.

Your child might enjoy making up new rhymes for each problem, or he might love to build each scene out of playdough.

STORY PROBLEMS:
The goal behind including story problems is to build fluency with math procedures; after all, the point of learning math facts is to be able to use them in real life. As you read the problems to the student(s), have them draw stick figures and coins to represent what you say.

1- "How would you solve this? Multiplication or division? Ben and Jane saved their allowance for the whole summer. By September, they had $24.00 all together. How much money did each child have?" **(For this problem, have them draw stick figures, then draw a pile of money representing $24. As you ask the question, have them study what they drew. Answer: Division.)**

2- "How would you solve this? Multiplication or division? Jack washed cars on Saturday and earned $2.00 for each car he washed. Altogether, he washed 8 cars. How much money did he earn?" **(For this problem, they could either draw 8 cars or use circles to represent cars. If they put $2 inside each car, they will study what they drew as they determine to multiply to solve this problem.)**

PRACTICE PROBLEMS:
Use sheet 3.3 from page 102.

4 GIANT TWELVES

Our two ladies in this picture each have a story to tell. They are going to show us that 12s are really great to look at after learning 2s. The last time we talked, Miss 2 had gone for a walk searching for doubles—and she'd found a lot of them! Today she decided to take her friend Agent 1 for a walk. Miss 2 had told her about the enormous hen she'd seen with the shelves of eggs, and Agent 1 was really anxious to meet her.

Chart for 12x

12 x 1 = 12	12 x 2 = 24	12 x 3 = 36	12 x 4 = 48	12 x 5 = 60
12 x 6 = 72	12 x 7 = 84	12 x 8 = 96	12 x 9 = 108	12 x 10 = 120
12 x 11 = 132	12 x 12 = 144			

But first, notice in this chart that three of the boxes are colored blue. This is because these are problems you already know. Notice the number patterns in each column of answers. Just like in the 2x chart, each column of numbers end the same, and they count up by 2s. See how many number patterns you can find.

Anyway, the friends decided to visit the giant hen. The friends introduced themselves and found that the hen's name was Henormous. ("That is surely fitting," breathed Agent 1 to Miss 2.) Henormous invited them in. They saw two nests each holding 6 eggs.

Henormous said she had gotten very busy because a lot of people wanted to buy the eggs from her egg business. She couldn't have just one shelf with nests on it anymore. She had to have a lot of them!

Henormous showed the ladies another area where she had two shelves each holding 12 eggs—10 brown and 2 white. They could see that there were two 10s made of the brown eggs and four 1s left over which were the white eggs. This shows that 2 x 12 = two 10s and two 2s.

2 x 12 = 24 which means 2 tens and 4 ones

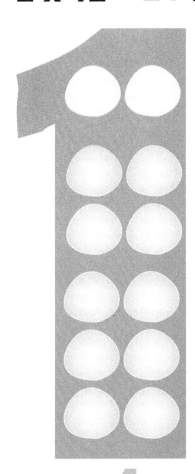

NOTE TO TEACHER:

These first illustrations are to show the student(s) that 12s are made of a 10 and two 1s. They will see the visuals of the brown and white eggs with the brown eggs representing the 10s place and the remaining white eggs representing the 1s place. So for example, three 12s will have three 10s, and each 10 will have 2 white eggs beside it which in this case turns out to be 6 white eggs.

For 12 x 4, there will be four 10s and 4 x 2 (8) white eggs for an answer of 48. For numbers over 4 there is a special trick.

We will transition to a story led by the friends, Agent 1 and Miss 2, to show the student(s) a shortcut for learning 12s by recalling 2s.

A great hands-on activity is to use empty egg cartons with colored plastic eggs to build 12x problems. Use one color egg for the 10s and a different color for the 1s. This activity will help the child(ren) understand visually what is happening with 12x problems.

(See also NOTE TO TEACHER on the bottom of page 46.)

Then they saw 3 shelves with a dozen eggs on each one—10 brown and 2 white just like before. They could see that there were three 10s this time made out of the brown eggs and six 1s left over made of the white eggs. So 3 x 12 = three 10s and six 1s.

3 x 12 = 36 which means 3 tens and 6 ones

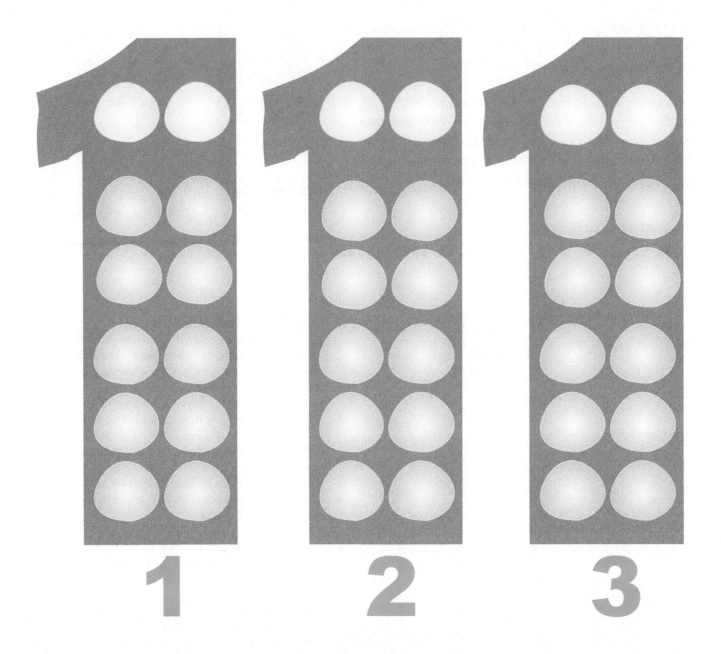

Suddenly Miss 2 got really excited. She remembered her walk from the day before and all the doubles she'd seen. She thought that 2 x 2 and 12 x 2 were very much alike. Let's look at what she realized as she dragged Agent 1 back to the first two shelves they saw holding two dozen eggs.

2 x 2 = 4

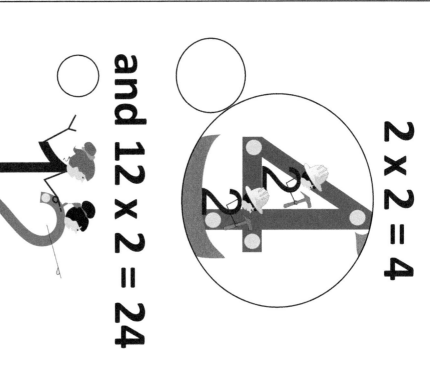

and 12 x 2 = 24

"Yesterday when I went walking, I saw two workers on a big purple boat. That was a picture of 2 x 2. Now I see 12 x 2 and the picture is almost the same!

Start with 2 x 2 = 4, and then for 12 x 2, one worker steps off the boat and stands beside it to make a 24."

2 x 3 = 6

and 12 x 3 = 36

"2 x 3 reminds me of 12 x 3!

Start with 2 x 3 = 6, and for 12 x 3, one Triple Mouse climbs out of the house and stands beside it."

2 x 4 = 8

and 12 x 4 = 48

"2 x 4 reminds me of 12 x 4!

Start with 2 x 4 = 8, and for 12 x 4, one boat is dragged to shore to sit by the lakes."

2 x 5 = 10

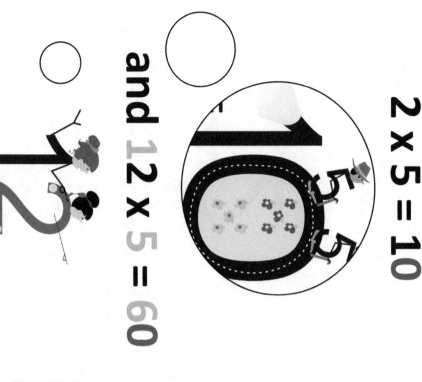

and 12 x 5 = 60

Remember that Agent 1 is a detective. She noticed something when they got to 12 x 5. "Miss 2, I just noticed that we can do 2 x 5 first and get a 10. But this time when we do 12 x 5 and Mr. 5 goes to stand by the park, he bumps into the light post! Let's just make Mr. 5 and the light post one number. Let's add them together to make a 6!"

Notice in "and 12 x 5 = 60" that if you pick up the green 5 and add it to the green 1 you get a green 6 in the 60. When you see 12 x 5, solve 2 x 5 = 10 first. Just write the 0 on your paper and hold out one finger. Add the 5 to your finger and then write the 6).

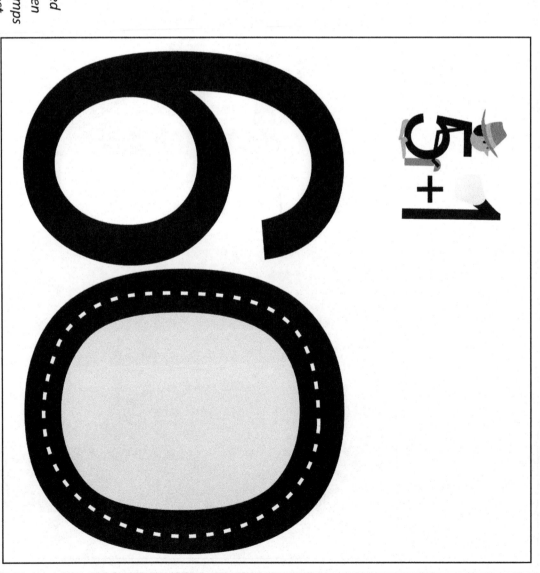

2 x 6 = 12

and 12 x 6 = 72

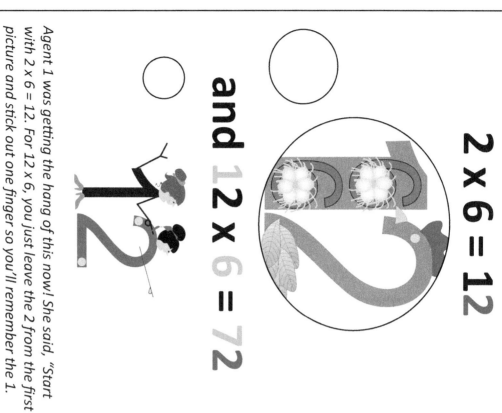

Agent 1 was getting the hang of this now! She said, "Start with 2 x 6 = 12. For 12 x 6, you just leave the 2 from the first picture and stick out one finger so you'll remember the 1. Now you notice that one nest fell off the shelf! Add that 6 nest to your finger to make 7. So 12 x 6 is just like 2 x 6 except the first number in the answer is one bigger than 6."

Also notice that in "and 12 x 6 = 72," adding the green 1 to the green 6 makes the green 7 in 72.

2 x 7 = 14

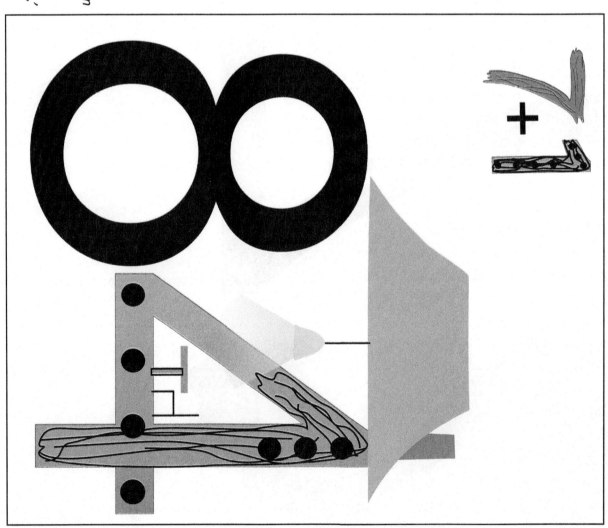

and 12 x 7 = 84

"I want to do this one!" said Miss 2. "For 12 x 7, start out with the 14 from 2 x 7, but a wooden 7 comes out to stand beside the 1 and gets all mixed with it. Next thing we know, there's an 8 by the 4!"

"Good one," said Agent 1. "Also notice that in 'and 12 x 7 = 84,' adding the green 1 to the green 7 makes the green 8 in 84."

2 x 8 = 16

and 12 x 8 = 96

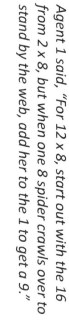

Agent 1 said, "For 12 x 8, start out with the 16 from 2 x 8, but when one 8 spider crawls over to stand by the web, add her to the 1 to get a 9."

Also notice that in "and 12 x 8 = 96," adding the green 1 to the green 8 makes the green 9 in 96.

2 x 9 = 18

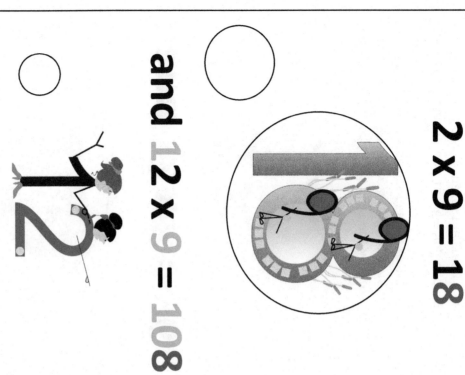

and 12 x 9 = 108

"For 12 x 9, start out with the 18 from 2 x 9, but I can plainly see that someone tied one 9 balloon to the 1 in 18. If you add them together, you would change the 1 in 18 to a 10," said Miss 2.

Also notice that in "and 12 x 9 = 108," adding the green 1 to the green 9 makes the green 10 in 108.

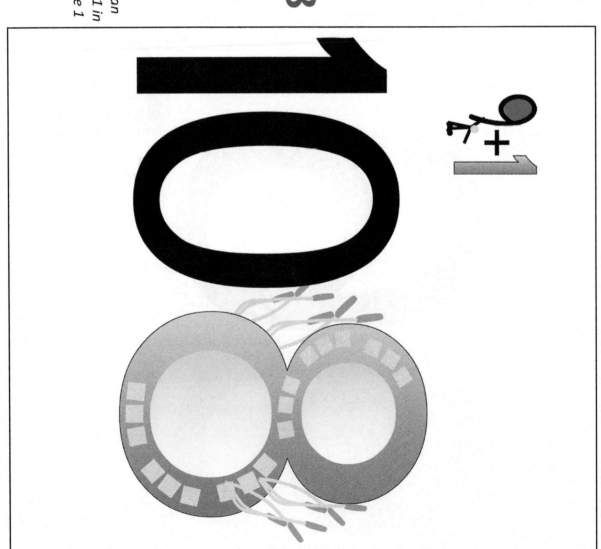

"12 x 11 is easy," the ladies thought. And for 12 x 10 they remembered Mr. 10 tossing a colored ring. "12 x 12 got carried away," they thought, "because he doubled the number in the 1s place 2 times!"

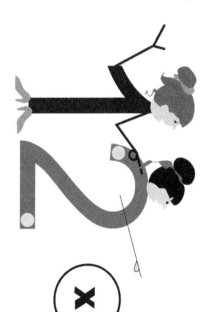

Mr. 10 tosses a colored ring.

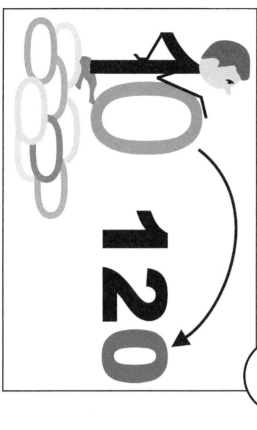

Add the 1+2 and put it in the middle!

1 then double 2, double 2.

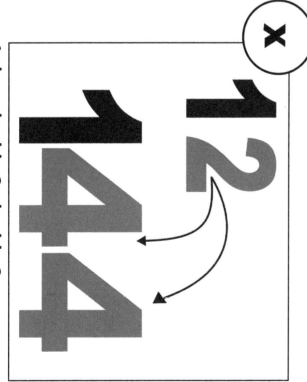

45

LOOKING FOR PATTERNS

Let's look at the answers to the 12s to see if we can find some patterns that will help our 12s be memorable.

HERE THEY ARE:

1x 12	2x 24	3x 36	4x 48	5x 60
6x 72	7x 84	8x 96	9x 108	10x 120
11x 132	12x 144			

HUNTING FOR PATTERNS:

• The first thing I notice is that in the 1s place, we count up by 2s: 2, 4, 6, 8, (1)0.

• I notice that both 5 x 12 and 10 x 12 end in a 0. Also, if we look at the columns, the numbers in the first column end the same, the numbers in the 2nd column end the same, etc.

• Notice that in the 10s place, we start counting up one number at a time until we reach 5x. Then we skip a number and go from 4 to 6. We continue on the second row counting up a number at a time (in the 10s and 100s place) until we get to 10x, and again we skip a number, going from 10 to 12.

• I think it is really interesting that in row 1, for 1x through 4x, Agent 1 says "Just be yourself" to the number in the 10s place, while Miss 2 is doubling the numbers in the 10s place to get the numbers in the 1s place.

• Then from 6x through 9x in row 2, the number in the 10s place is one more than the original number. For example, 8 x 12 = 96. The 9 is one digit bigger than the 8. In row 3, the first 2 digits are 2 bigger than the 11x and 12x numbers. Miss 2 makes the 1s end like the double of the #x. For example, in 6 x 12 = 72, the answer ends the same way that double 6 ends (12). 7 x 12 = 84, the answer ends the same way as double 7 (14), etc.

PRACTICE PROBLEMS:
Use sheet 4.1 from page 103.

NOTE TO TEACHER:
This chapter describes many ways to look at 12x. They are not intended to be mind-numbing exercises for the student(s). However, we all see things differently, and each student will prefer one of these ways of solving for 12 more than another. If she is strongly visual, the images will help. If he relies on patterns, the chart above will help. Some students will easily learn to solve for 12x the traditional way, only to forget how in a week. For this reason we have included the tricks, the relationship to the 2x table, etc.

STILL ANOTHER WAY TO DO 12x

Let's use the "wall and line" method to help us learn our 12s another way. We also need to keep in mind what the digits mean. The 1 in 12 means "One 10." The 2 in 12 means "Two 1s."

This is what the problems look like:

12 x 1 = Means 1 x 10 & 1 x 2	10 + 2 12
12 x 2 = Means 2 x 10 & 2 x 2	20 + 4 24
12 x 3 = Means 3 x 10 & 3 x 2	30 + 6 36
12 x 4 = Means 4 x 10 & 4 x 2	40 + 8 48
12 x 5 = Means 5 x 10 & 5 x 2	50 +10 60
12 x 6 = Means 6 x 10 & 6 x 2	60 +12 72

12 x 7 = Means 7 x 10 & 7 x 2	70 +14 84
12 x 8 = Means 8 x 10 & 8 x 2	80 +16 96
12 x 9 = Means 9 x 10 & 9 x 2	90 +18 108
12 x 10 = Means 10 x 10 & 10 x 2	100 + 20 120
12 x 11 = Means 11 x 10 & 11 x 2	110 + 22 132
12 x 12 = Means 12 x 10 & 12 x 2	120 + 24 144

 When you divide 12, 24, 36 and 48 by 12, just take the number in the 10s place as the answer!

12 ÷ 12 = __1__   24 ÷ 12 = __2__   36 ÷ 12 = __3__   48 ÷ 12 = __4__

For numbers 60, 72, 84, 96 and 108, the answer will be one less than the 10s number:

60 ÷ 12 = __5__   72 ÷ 12 = __6__   84 ÷ 12 = __7__   96 ÷ 12 = __8__   108 ÷ 12 = __9__

For numbers 120-168, the answer will be 2 numbers smaller than the first two numbers:

120 ÷ 12 = __10__   132 ÷ 12 = __11__   144 ÷ 12 = __12__

PRACTICE PROBLEMS:
Use sheet 4.2 from page 103.

Tactile and kinesthetic activities for learning 12s

FOR ANYONE:

To make this a fully tactile lesson, use plastic numbers to create the problems. Child(ren) will lay out each problem like this:

12 x 1 = 1 and double 1 (2)

12 x 2 = 2 and double 2 (4)

12 x 3 = 3 and double 3 (6)

12 x 4 = 4 and double 4 (8)

To find the answer for 12 x 1 through 12 x 4, the child(ren) will just move the multiplier over to the answer spot to the right, find the number that is double the multiplier and place it just after to form the 2-digit answer. For example, with 12 x 2 =, move the 2 to the right and find a 4 to put after it, because 4 is double 2. For 12 x 4, move the 4 to the right and find its double (8) to put after it, making 48.

To find the answers for problems 12 x 5 through 12 x 9, the child(ren) will place the answers to 2x those same numbers (5–9); then they will add the multiplier to the 10s place to arrive at the correct answer. If they are physically picking up the numbers that they are adding and replacing them with the correct number in the 10s place, it will reinforce what is happening in the math problem.

To bring this lesson full circle, have the child(ren) draw their own illustrations of the problems of the shelves, nests, and eggs. Or they may create the problem by modeling with playdough.

STORY PROBLEMS:

1- "How would you solve this? Multiplication or division? Henormous got 6 egg cartons and put 12 eggs in each one. How many eggs did she use in all?" (Multiplication)

2- "How would you solve this? Multiplication or division? Henormous had 96 eggs. She sold them to 12 customers. How many eggs did each customer get?" (Division)

PRACTICE PROBLEMS:
Use sheet 4.3 from page 104.

HIGH FIVES

You can learn a ton about 5s from your own two hands. If you do high fives with a friend, both your fives together make a ten. Your hand by itself, of course, is just a five.

5s are cool because we use them a lot for counting money, for telling time, and for all sorts of other really useful activities.

Remember from Chapter 3 that two Mr. 5s went walking on the track around the park. In the park were two patches of flowers with five flowers in each patch.

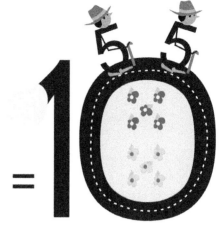

Chart for 5x				
5 x 1 = 5	5 x 2 = 10	5 x 3 = 15	5 x 4 = 20	5 x 5 = 25
5 x 6 = 30	5 x 7 = 35	5 x 8 = 40	5 x 9 = 45	5 x 10 = 50
5 x 11 = 55	5 x 12 = 60			

Notice in this chart that you already know five of the boxes. That leaves us with only 7 combinations to learn! Study the chart for a bit and see what patterns you can discover in the array of numbers.

In this High Fives chapter, we will use dominoes that look a lot like the flower beds in the park.

The square is a 5, while the rectangle is a 10:

Whenever you see the square, you can think about 1 x 5. Whenever you see the rectangle, you can think about two 5s, or a 10 (2 x 5 = 10).

Use body motions for 5s and 10s to deepen learning.

Body motions for 5s and 10s:

claps for 10s; fist for 5s

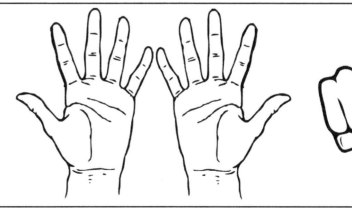

49

MULTIPLYING 5s

1 x 5 = 5

ODD NUMBERS:

When you have 5 x an odd number, the answer will always end in a 5.

3 x 5 = 15

5 x 5 = 25

7 x 5 = 35

9 x 5 = 45

11 x 5 = 55

EVEN NUMBERS:

2 x 5 = 10

When you have 5 x an even number, the answer will always end in a 0 because you are making tens, and tens end with 0.

4 x 5 = 20

You can remember even numbers x 5 because you can take half of the number x 10:

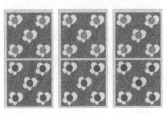

6 x 5 = 30

2x5 is 1 ten
4x5 is 2 tens
6x5 is 3 tens
8x5 is 4 tens
10x5 is 5 tens
12x5 is 6 tens

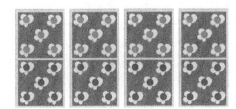

8 x 5 = 40

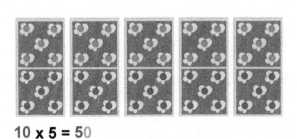

10 x 5 = 50

12 x 5 = 60

THINKING ABOUT 5s

Think about the pictures you just saw. Can you see the pictures in your head as you think about each 5x problem? Think about what the dominoes will look like for each problem.

For EVEN NUMBERS such as 6 x 5 =   If you first make 10s, as many as you can, you will easily arrive at the answer. Counting 5s by 2s is like making 10s. So for 6 x 5, count "2, 4, 6" sticking one finger out for each number, and you find that you have made three 10s or 30. So 5 x 6 = 30.

For ODD NUMBERS such as 9 x 5 =   If you start counting by 2s, you'll say "2, 4, 6, 8" and you will have made four 10s and have a 5 left over to make 45. For 7 x 5, count 2, 4, 6 and make three 10s. You will have one 5 left over to make 35 in all.

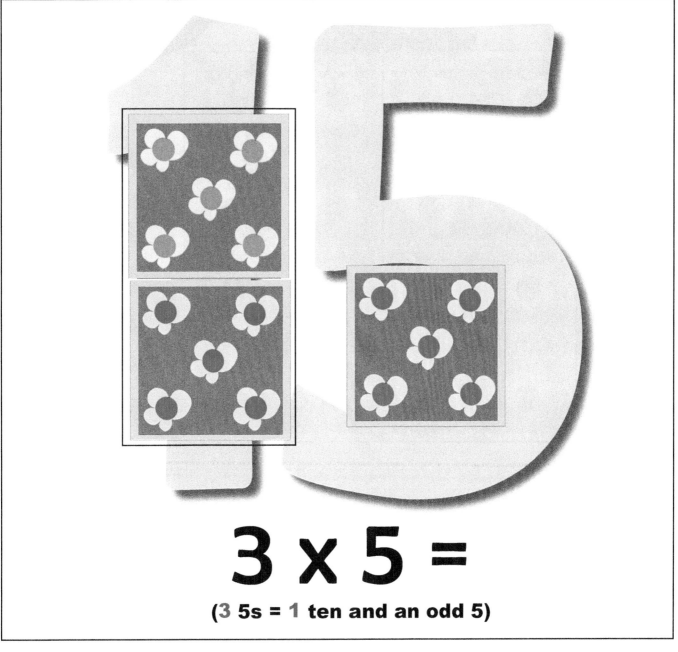

3 x 5 =

(3 5s = 1 ten and an odd 5)

20

4 x 5 =

(4 5s = 2 tens)

5 x 5 =

(5 5s = 2 tens and an odd 5)

30

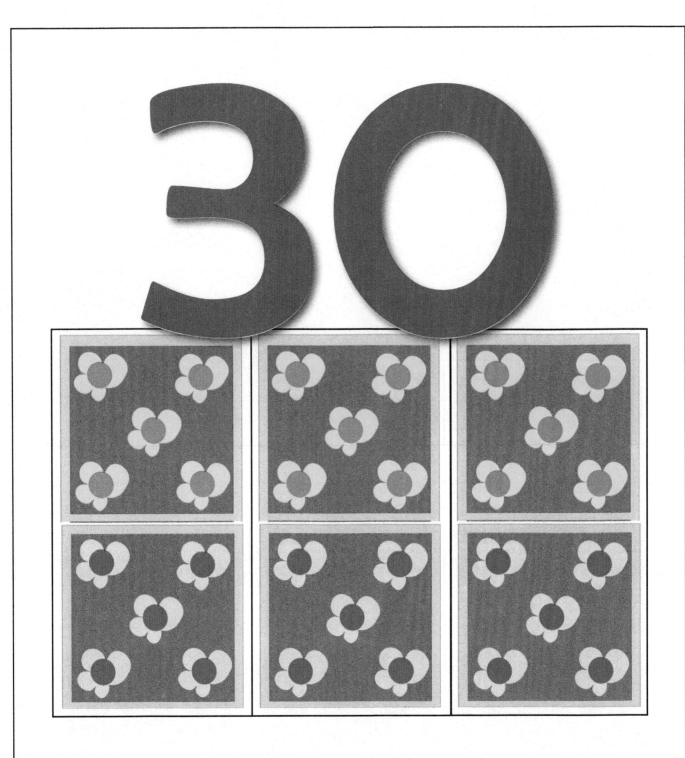

6 x 5 =

(6 5s = 3 tens)

7 x 5 =

(7 5s = 3 tens and an odd 5)

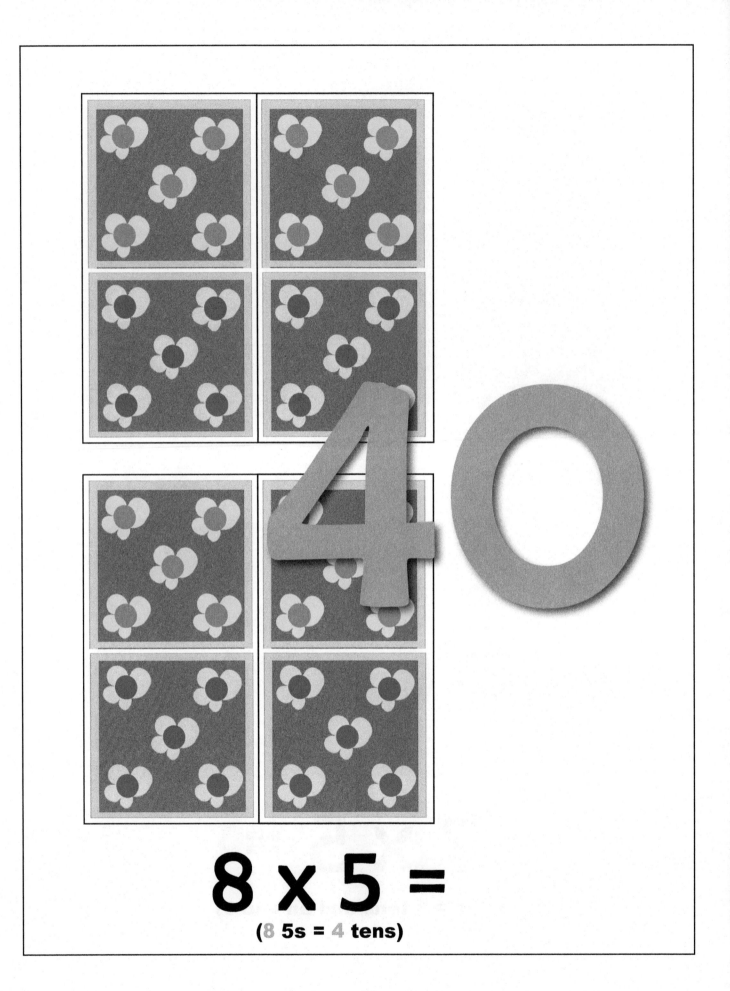

8 x 5 =

(8 5s = 4 tens)

9 x 5 =

(9 5s = 4 tens and an odd 5)

PRACTICE PROBLEMS:
Use sheet 5.1 from page 105.

Dividing by 5s is fun when you think about how to make it simple.

Let's look at the answers to all the multiplication problems we had in the first part of this chapter. Here they are:

5, 10, 15, 20, 25, 30, 35, 40, 45, 50, 55, 60

FOR EVEN NUMBERS:

To divide by 5 all the numbers that end in a 0, all you have to do is cover the 0 and double the number that is left. *You double the number because every 10 has two 5s in it!*

For example:

> **40 ÷ 5 = (Cover the 0, leaving the 4. Now double the 4 and you have 8.)**
> **So, 40 ÷ 5 = 8**

HANDS-ON:
Take a piece of scratch paper. Make a column of these numbers: 10, 20, 30, 40, 50, 60, 70, 80, 90, 100, 110, 120. You will be dividing by 5. Cover the zero with your finger and double the number that is left to get your answer. Remember, there are double the 5s in each number.

FOR ODD NUMBERS:

Let's look at the answers ending in 5 now.

5, 15, 25, 35, 45, 55

For these problems, instead of covering the 5 at the end like you did the 0 on the even numbers, you will take off the final 5, but you will need to stick one finger out to remind you that you took off a five. Next, look at the number that is left and double it. Then add the one finger to it.

For example:

> **25 ÷ 5 = (Take off the 5 and hold out one finger. 2 is left. Double the 2 to get 4 and then add the 1 from your finger to the 4.)**
> **The answer to 25 ÷ 5 is 5 (double 2 = 4 + 1 finger = 5)**

HANDS-ON:
Take a piece of scratch paper. Make a column of the numbers that end in 5 (see above). You will be dividing by 5. Cover the 5 with your finger and double the number that is left; then, add the 1 to get your answer.

PRACTICE PROBLEMS:
Use sheet 5.2 from page 105.

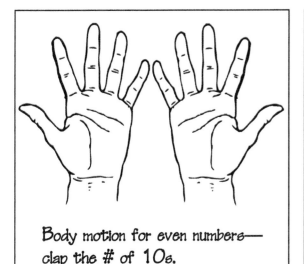

Body motion for even numbers— clap the # of 10s.

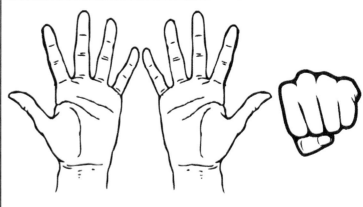

Body motion for odds—claps for 10s and a fist for the final 5.

Tactile and kinesthetic activities for learning 5s

This activity will involve clapping and chanting. Child(ren) will say their 5x facts, clapping out the answer.

Say, "1 times 5 is 5." Make a fist as you say 5.
"2 x 5 = 10" Clap once as you say 10.
"3 x 5 = 15" Say "fif- (clap) teen (fist)."
"4 x 5 = 20" Say "twen- (slap legs) ty (clap)."
"5 x 5 = 25" Say "twen- (slap legs) ty (clap) five (fist)."
"6 x 5 = 30" Say "thir- (slap legs) (clap) ty (clap)."
"7 x 5 = 35" Say "thir- (slap legs) (clap) ty (clap) five (fist)."
"8 x 5 = 40" Say "for- (slap legs) (clap) ty (slap legs) (clap)."
"9 x 5 = 45" Say "for- (slap legs) (clap) ty (slap legs) (clap)" five (fist)."
"10 x 5 = 50" Say "fif- (slap legs) (clap) (clap) ty (slap legs) (clap)."
"11 x 5 = 55" Say "fif- (slap legs) (clap) (clap) ty (slap legs) (clap) five (fist)."
"12 x 5 = 60" Say "six- (slap legs) (clap) (clap) ty (slap legs) (clap) (clap)."

STORY PROBLEMS:

1- "How would you solve this? Multiplication or division? The garden club decided they needed to plant new flower beds in the park. 6 people showed up on Saturday to make the flower beds. By the end of the day, each person had planted 5 beds. How many new beds were made?" (Multiplication)

2- "How would you solve this? Multiplication or division? During May, the garden club made 45 flower beds. If each person made 5 beds, how many people worked on the flower beds?" (Division)

PRACTICE PROBLEMS:
Use sheet 5.3 from page 106.

NIFTY NINE

me

1x

Nine is pretty stuck on himself, I think. You will probably see what I mean in a minute. He used to be a red balloon, but he got so famous that he became a movie star.

Mr. 9 loves, loves, loves his number. He arranged his table so that all the answers add up to his name—9. Let's take a look.

Notice in this chart that six of the boxes are colored blue. This is because these are problems you already know. See how many number patterns you can find.

Chart for 9x				
9 x 1 = 9	9 x 2 = 18	9 x 3 = 27	9 x 4 = 36	9 x 5 = 45
9 x 6 = 54	9 x 7 = 63	9 x 8 = 72	9 x 9 = 81	9 x 10 = 90
9 x 11 = 99	9 x 12 = 108			

You might notice that the answer to a number times 9 will start with a digit smaller... oh let me just show you an example: 4 x 9 = 36. You start the answer with 1 number less than the 4 and then the second number is the number that goes with the 3 to make a 9. (This works for all the 9x except for 9 x 11 which is two 9s.) For 9 x 12, add 1 + 0 + 8 and, voila, you have another 9!

5 x 9 = 45 (4 is 1 number less than 5, and 4 + 5 = 9)

6 x 9 = 54 (5 is 1 less than 6, and 5 + 4 = 9)

7 x 9 = the number 1 less than 7 _____ plus what goes with it to make 9? _____ (3)

8 x 9 = _____ (72)   9 x 9 = _____ (81) YAY!

Just remember this phrase: "Make a 9." You will need it for this whole chapter!

MORE EXAMPLES:

4 x 9 = *36* _____ (3 is 1 less than 4. 3 + 6 = 9. Answer is 36).

2 x 9 = *18* _____   8 x 9 = *72* _____

PRACTICE PROBLEMS:
Use sheet 6.1 from page 107.

9 x 2

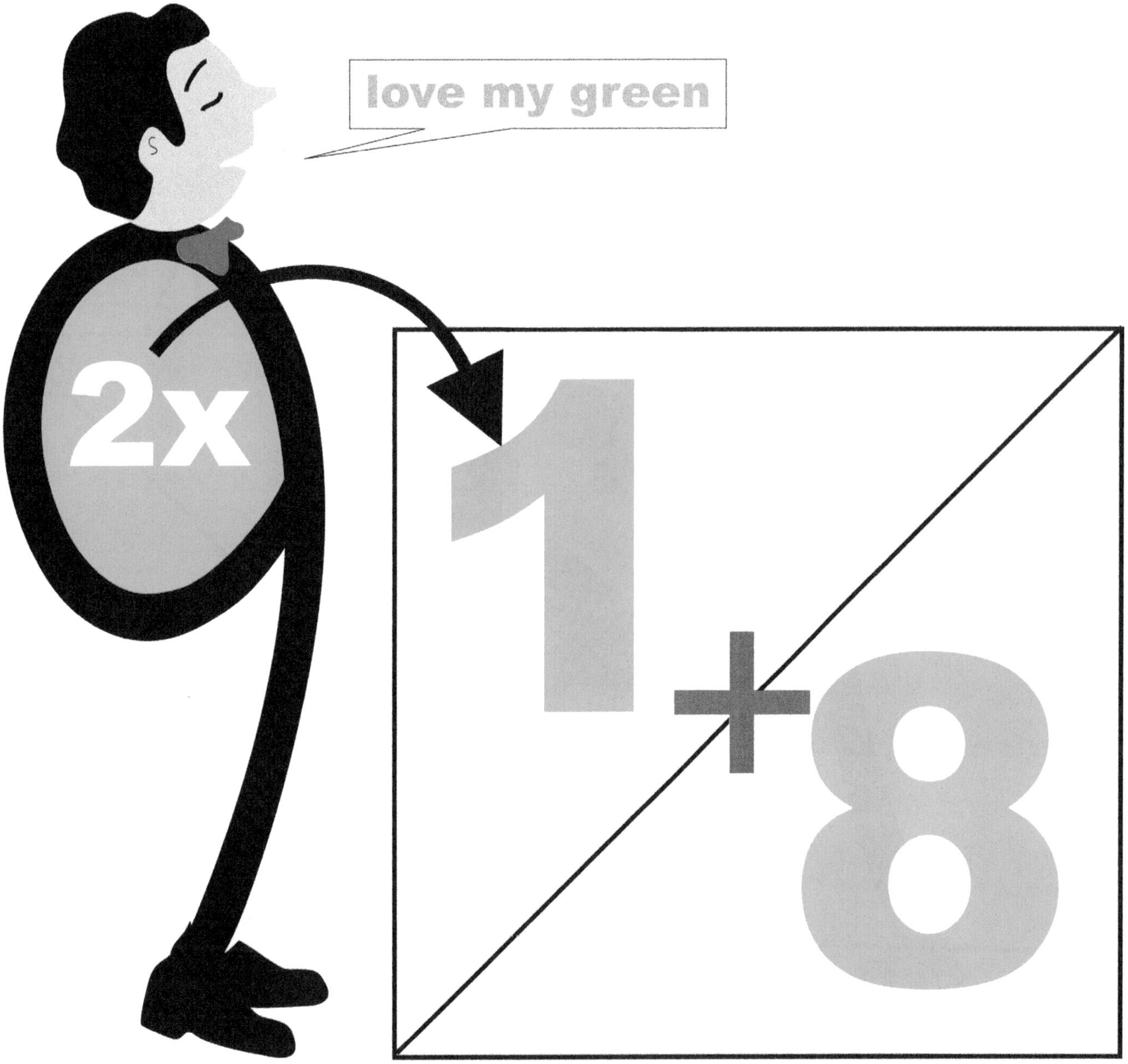

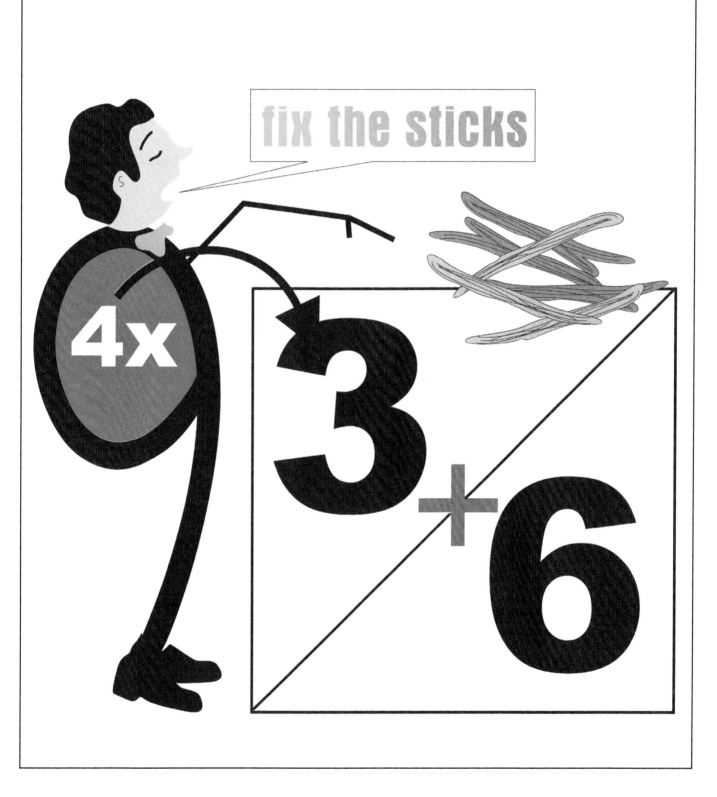

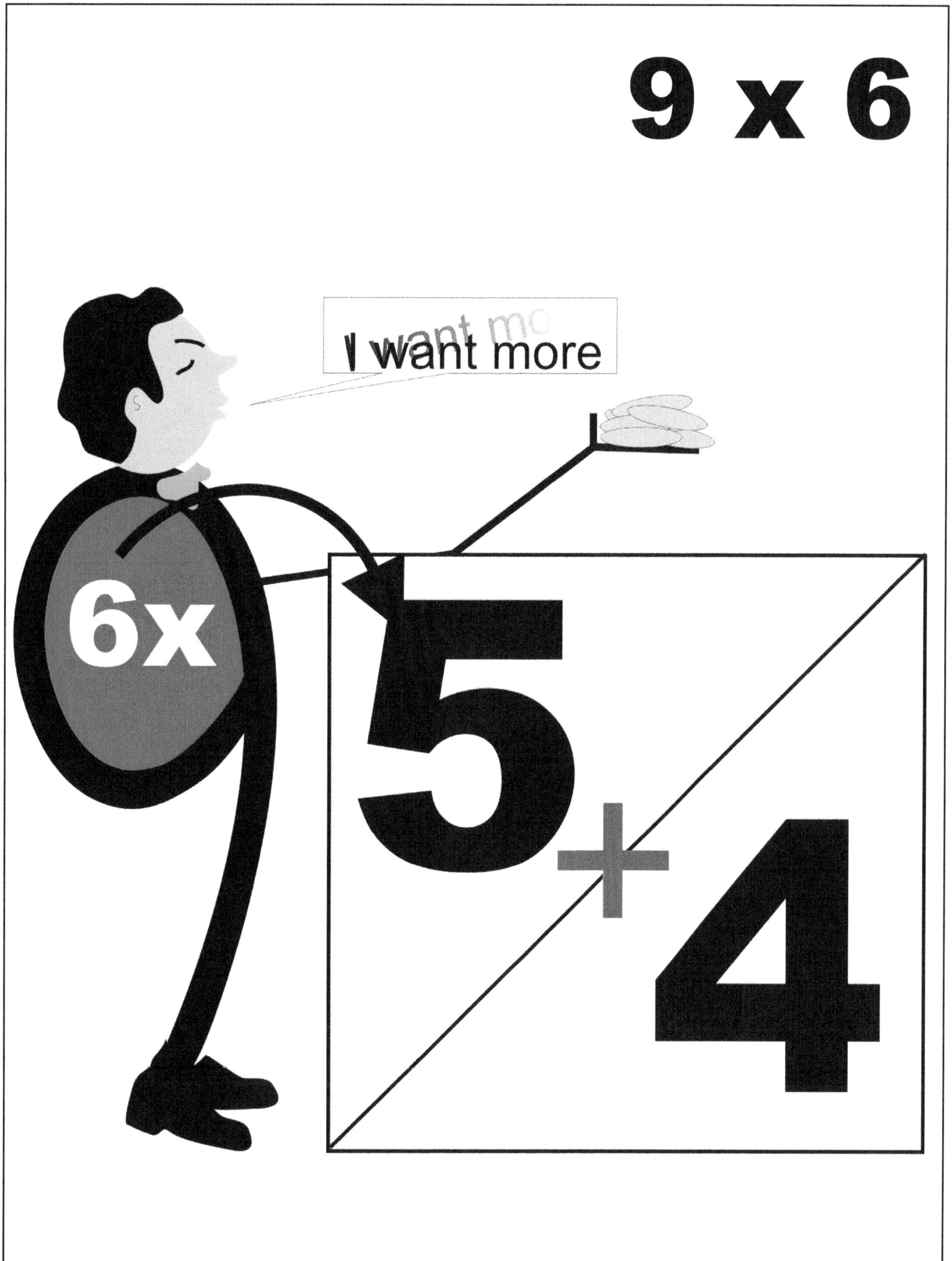
9 x 6
I want more
6x
5
+
4

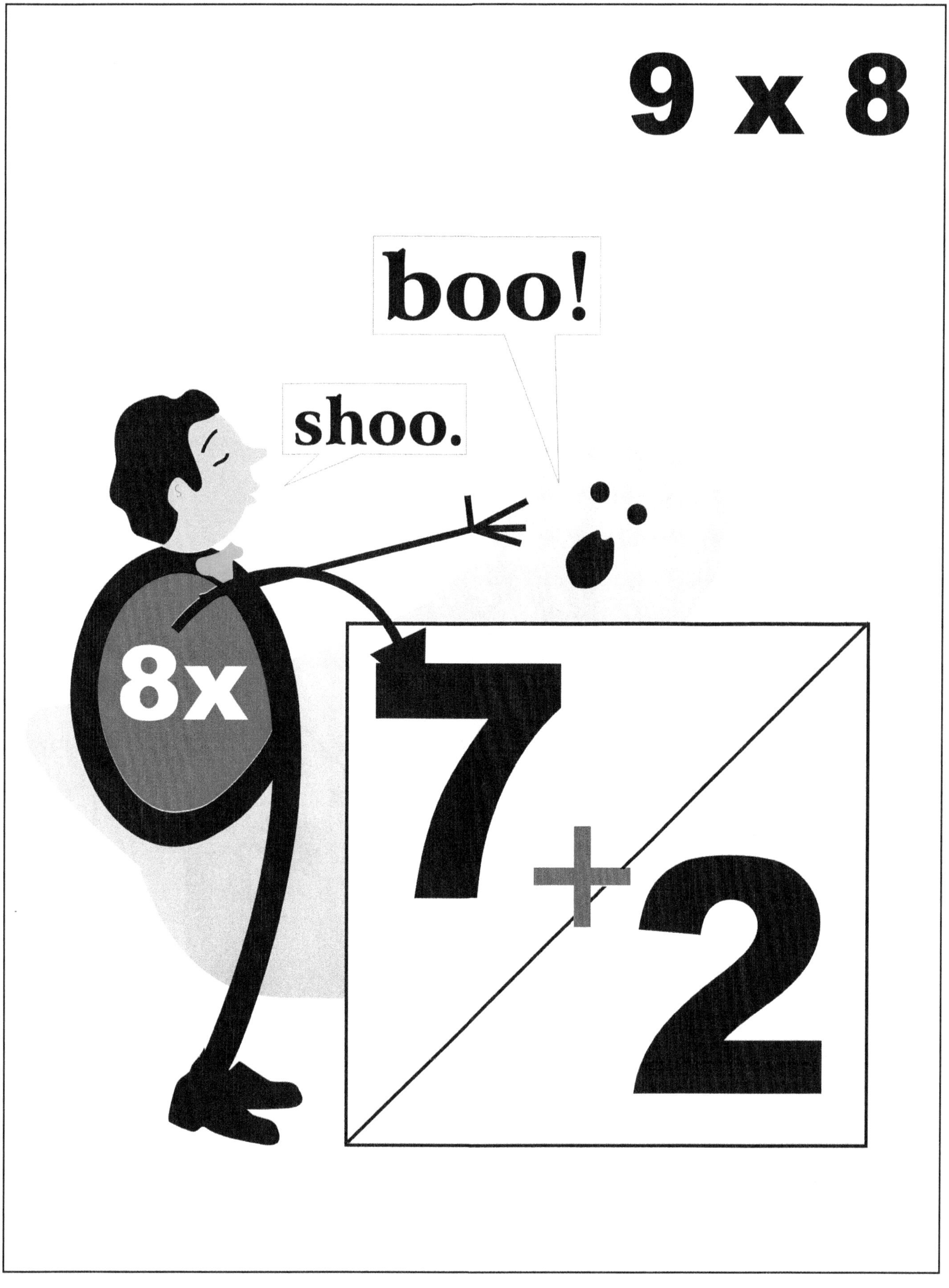
9 x 8
boo!
shoo.
8x
7
+
2

For each problem, look at the first number in the dividend. With the dividends for 9 x 2 through 9 x 8, the answer will be one more than that first digit.

FOR EXAMPLE:

36 ÷ 9 = 4 (one digit larger than the 3 in 36).
45 ÷ 9 = 5 (one digit larger than the 4 in 45).

For 9 ÷ 1, remember Agent 1 saying, "Just be yourself."
For 9 ÷ 9, the answer is 1 because any digit divided by itself is Agent 1 ("Just be yourself).
For 90 ÷ 9, just remember the colored ring from 9 x 10.
And for 99 ÷ 9, remember the double agent.
The only three digit dividend for 9s is the result of 12 x 9 (108).

HANDS-ON:
Take a piece of scratch paper. Make a column with these numbers: 72, 18, 45, 27, 54, 90, 99, 81, 108. Divide by 9. For 72 ÷ 9 through 18 ÷ 9, remember to cover the second number and make the remaining number 1 bigger than itself.

YOUR TWO HANDS:
You may also use your hands to do your 9s table (1 x 9 through 9 x 9), if you prefer.

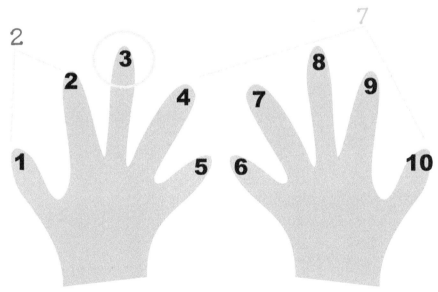

If you are multiplying 3 x 9, tuck your number 3 finger down. (See that finger 3 is circled.) What you have left is 2 numbers to the left and 7 numbers to the right of the 3 that you tucked down. So 3 x 9 = 27.

Multiply 7 x 9. Tuck down the 7 finger and you will have 6 fingers on the left and 3 on the right of the 7. So the answer to 7 x 9 is 63.

HANDS-ON:
Take a piece of scratch paper. Write the numbers from 1–9 mixed up in a column. Multiply by 9 and use your hands as we talked about just above.

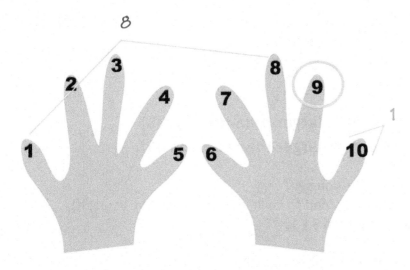

FOR DIVISION:
When you see a dividend such as 81, make that number on your hands and the answer will be the finger that is tucked under (or circled, as in this illustration).

DIVIDING BY 9:

Once you can multiply by 9, dividing is super easy.

Do these problems using your two hands:

36 ÷ 9 = (the number between a group of 3 fingers and 6 fingers is finger #4)

72 ÷ 9 = (the number between a group of 7 fingers and 2 fingers is finger #8)

81 ÷ 9 = (the number between a group of 8 fingers and 1 finger is finger #9)

HANDS-ON:
Take a piece of scratch paper. Write these numbers: 72, 27, 18, 63, 81, 36, 45. Divide by 9 using the two hands method shown above.

PRACTICE PROBLEMS:
Use sheet 6.2 from page 107.

Tactile and kinesthetic activities for learning 9s

FOR ANYONE:

This activity will involve becoming very familiar with the sums to 9. Without this fluency, the times table for 9 will not be easy.

Use the child(ren)'s choice of tactile numbers for the sums to 9—such as plastic magnetic numbers, colored paper numbers, etc. The primary function of this game is to get the child(ren) to see one number and automatically think of the number that goes with it. You can do this activity at home with one child or in the classroom in small math groups. For whole classroom, you could use pencil and paper and do this in the form of a quiz for fluency. You would need to write down your questions and have the children number their papers so you could do a quick check for correct answers later.

• Spread the numbers from 0–9 on the table. Mix them up.

• Call out one number (say 2). The child(ren) will grab that number and immediately grab the number that goes with it to make 9 (7). They will put those numbers back and mix the numbers again. Keep on calling one number at a time until you see that the child(ren) are not having to think about which numbers go together to make a 9.

• Next, go through the 9 minus problems. You will say "9 - 4" and the child(ren) will grab a 5. Keep on like this until you have gone through all the facts for 9- several times and the child(ren) are very comfortable with finding the missing number.

• Now, for multiplication, call out a problem such as 9 x 5. The child(ren) will grab the 4 and the 5 and place them on the table.

• And finally, for division, say a problem such as 45 ÷ 9, and the child(ren) will grab the 5.

STORY PROBLEMS:

1- "How would you solve this? Multiplication or division? Mr. and Mrs. Brown had 9 children who went to the store to buy candy. When they got home, they piled their candy on the kitchen table to split it up. When they counted the candy, they found there were 72 pieces. If each child got the same number of candies, how many would each child get?" (Division)

2- "How would you solve this? Multiplication or division? The Browns raised chickens and their children collected the eggs every day. Saturday, the 9 children went out to the henhouse. Each child found 7 eggs. How many eggs did they find in all?" (Multiplication)

PRACTICE PROBLEMS:
Use sheet 6.3 from page 108.

7 THREE BIG MICE, SEE HOW THEY RUN

Remember when Miss 2 went looking for doubles? She saw two huge mice living in a lavender house with a stick roof and six slabs of cheese to eat. They were so big she named them each Triple Mouse. Well, before too long, the mice began to multiply. Really, they did! Then their lavender house was far too small. The Triple Mice began to wander around looking for a larger, more suitable place to live.

Chart for 3x

3 x 1 = 3	3 x 2 = 6	3 x 3 = 9	3 x 4 = 12	3 x 5 = 15
3 x 6 = 18	3 x 7 = 21	3 x 8 = 24	3 x 9 = 27	3 x 10 = 30
3 x 11 = 33	3 x 12 = 36			

The colored boxes in this chart contain the answers we already know. Let's see. We did 3 x 1 or 1 x 3 already... We know seven of the problems already! Look at the little bit that is left to learn! In this chapter, you will need to study each picture, and then close your eyes, see the picture in your head, and describe what you see.

But now let's get back to Triple Mice and their search for a new home...

3 enormous mice suddenly appeared in the hot air man's hot air balloon! He nervously pointed to the sign that said "only 3 at a time." Even though he could plainly see there were only three Triple Mice, they were as big as 9 mice all together! Because the man was nervous, they climbed down and hurried away.
So remember, 3 Triple Mice (3s) = 9 regular mice.

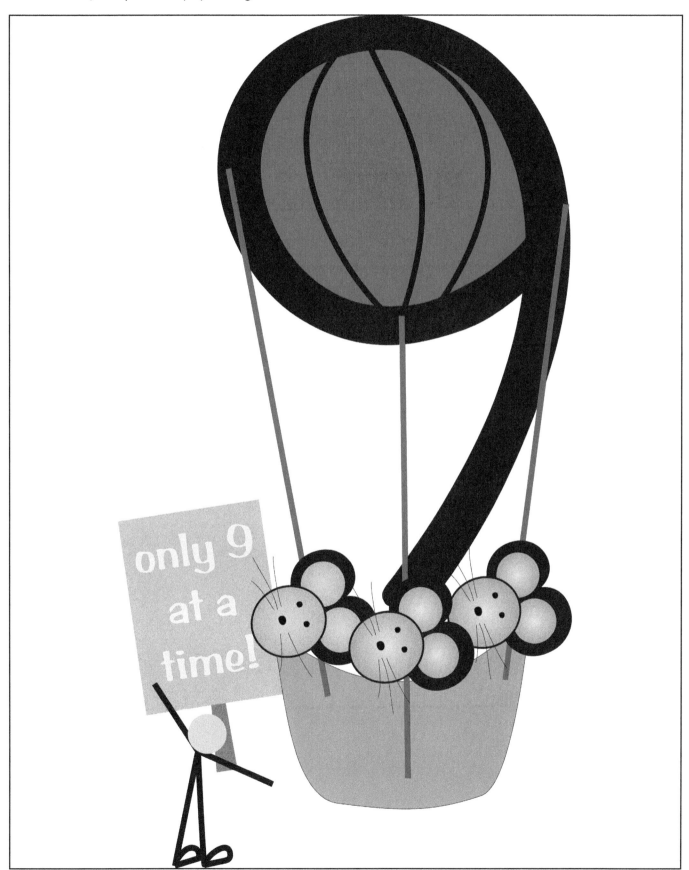

Imagine Henormous the Hen's surprise when she walked into her chicken house early the next morning. Something didn't look quite right. Actually, something looked very very strange! There sat 12 "eggs" on the shelf, but they looked a lot like four mice in disguise! Just between you and me... four mice had painted their faces and arranged themselves quietly on the shelf, hoping Henormous wouldn't notice!
4 Triple Mice (3s) = 12.

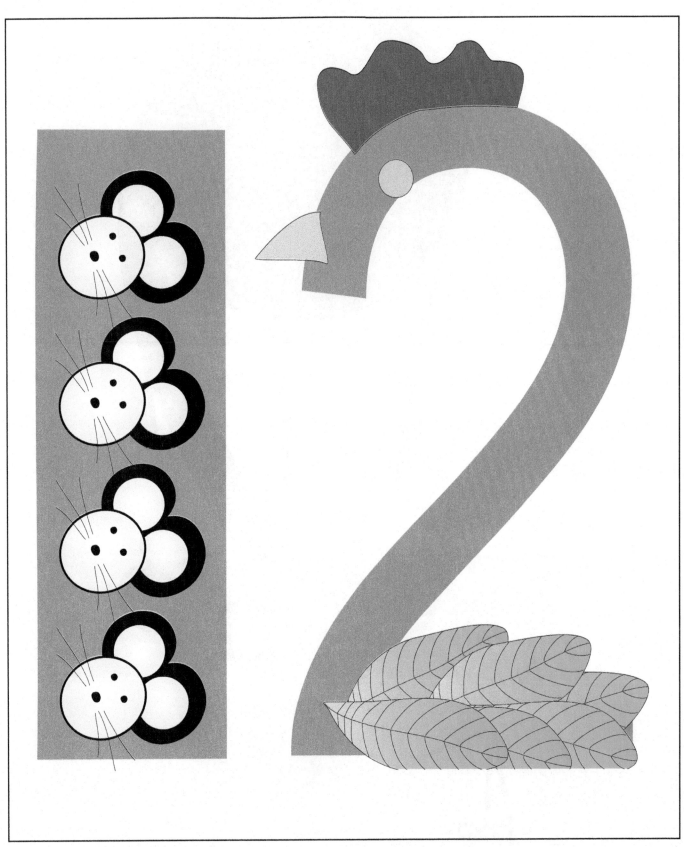

Later at the lakes, people who came hoping to go boating were shocked to find the lakes filled with big red boats and 3 Triple Mice in each boat. Altogether, 6 Triple Mice were as big and heavy as 18 mice. Pretty soon, the boats seemed like they might sink, so the mice quickly rowed to shore and waddled down the road in search of a new place to live. 6 Triple Mice (3s) = 18.

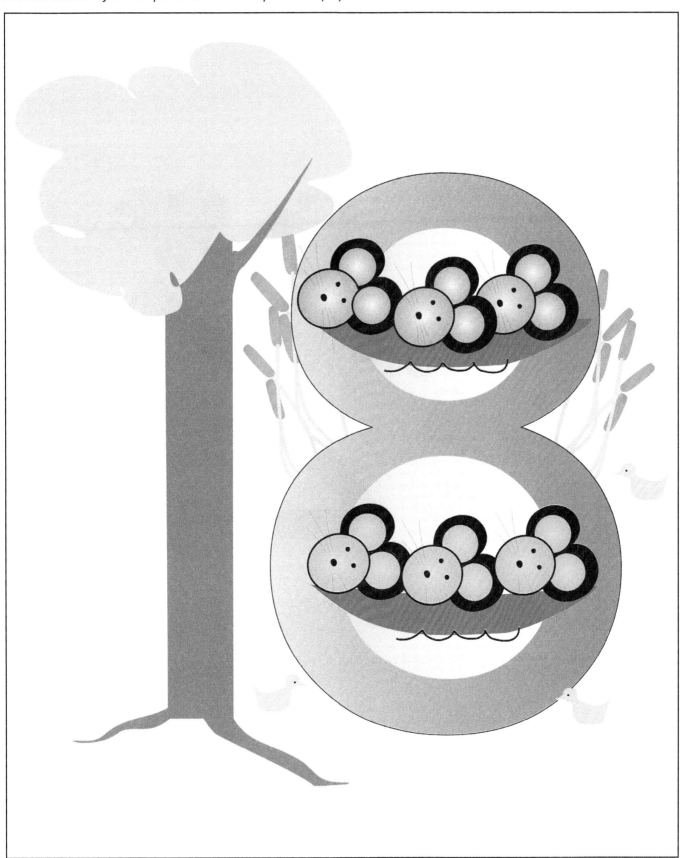

Miss 2 and Agent 1 kept hearing rumors of huge Triple Mice showing up unexpectedly, so they decided to find out what the ruckus was about. They set off down the road but never did find the mice. Of course if they had turned around, they would have seen 7 Triple Mice scuttling quietly after them! Even though there were only 7 Triple Mice, because they were so big, it looked like 21 mice following the friends down the road. 7 Triple Mice (3s) = 21.

Finally a kind soul decided to build the poor mice a nice big houseboat to live in. By this time she had to make a really huge boat because now there were 8 Triple Mice! They took up as much room as 24 mice would have! 8 Triple Mice (3s) = 24.

Tap, tap, saw, saw, tap, tap—before too long, the houseboat was completely done, and the mice moved in! Does it look a tiny bit crowded to you?

HANDS-ON:
Take a piece of scratch paper. Write these numbers: 9, 18, 24, 12, 21. Divide each one by 3. As you solve each problem, close your eyes and imagine the picture that goes with it.

PRACTICE PROBLEMS:
Use sheets 7.1–7.2 from page 109.

Tactile and kinesthetic activities for learning 3s

FOR ANYONE:

Chanting the 3 times table can be a bit rhythmic. "3, 6, 9, 12, 15, 18, 21, 24, 27, 30, (deep breath) 33, 36." As the child(ren) chant the table, they can hold up the number of fingers that go with each number. For example, with 3 they would hold up one finger, while with the 6, they would hold up two fingers.

Pattern discovery in the 3x chart is fun. Look at the chart together and notice that the numbers go up by three, of course, but the digit in the ones place has a pattern (pay attention to the color coding here. Read the red numbers first, then the blue, then the yellow.)

3, 6, 9, 12, 15, 18, 21, 24, 27

STORY PROBLEMS:
1- "How would you solve this? Multiplication or division? Mr. and Mrs. Brown had 9 children who earned their allowance by working around the home. Each child had 3 chores every day. How many chores did they do in all?" (I'll bet their house was always super clean!) (Multiplication)

2- "How would you solve this? Multiplication or division? Next door to the Browns lived the Greens. They had 3 children who also did chores around the house. Each day, 15 chores were done. How many chores did each child do at the Greens? Which family did do you think did more chores each, the Browns or the Greens?" (Division)

PRACTICE PROBLEMS:
Use sheet 7.3 from page 110.

FOUR, FOUR, SHUT THE DOOR

You are not going to believe what has been happening in the past several days. While we have been following the activities of Miss 2, the various Agents and Double Agents... not to mention the mice scurrying around to find a place to live...well, while all that was going on, we didn't notice how your multiplication/division chart has been melting away like butter on a hot sidewalk!

Here's the 4x chart:

Chart for 4x				
4 x 1 = 4	4 x 2 = 8	4 x 3 = 12	**4 x 4 = 16**	4 x 5 = 20
4 x 6 = 24	**4 x 7 = 28**	**4 x 8 = 32**	4 x 9 = 36	4 x 10 = 40
4 x 11 = 44	4 x 12 = 48			

I colored in the boxes containing the answers we already know. There are only four stories of 4s to talk about! In this chapter, remember to study the pictures, then close your eyes and talk about what you see.

In town was an old barn with huge swinging doors. The barn was mysterious because each time someone saw the doors, something very different was painted on them! And what was behind the doors was always a surprise, too.

One day Agent 1 saw that the doors of the barn had four boats painted on them. "I want to go boating today!" she said.

When she swung the doors open, she did see a boat, but it had a gigantic spiderweb and two red and green spiders climbing on it.

Agent 1 shivered and quietly closed the doors to the barn. "Four 4s all add up to a big cobwebby 16," she whispered to herself as she hurried away.

The next day, Agent 1 passed the barn and saw four nests with six eggs in each nest painted on the doors. "Today's my lucky day! I can get eggs for my cake here!" And she opened the doors shouting, "Henormous, I need to buy some eggs from you!"

While she did find Henormous... the giant hen was not tending nests nor laying eggs! She was about to go sailing on the lake!

"Let me go with you," cried Agent 1. So she forgot all about eggs and went sailing instead.

A week later, Agent 1 was looking for wood so she could make cake racks to hold her homemade cakes. As she passed the barn, she noticed four wooden 7s painted on the doors. "I should be able to find some great wood here," Agent 1 exclaimed as she hurried to open the doors.

But when Agent 1 opened the doors, she didn't see any wood. What Agent 1 saw was some tools on the ground by a new boat and Miss 2 waving goodbye to someone. "Well, I'll be!" said Agent 1. "They must have used up all the wood to build the boat! I guess I will have to try somewhere else."

A few days later, Agent 1 was looking everywhere for her friend Miss 2. She felt like going for a walk around the twin lakes. As she walked down the street she noticed the old barn had four pictures of twin lakes painted on the door.

"I doubt I will find Miss 2 OR the lakes here," said Agent 1 to herself. "There will probably be piles of rusty cars. Or huge spiders. Or bee hives or stacks of lumber. Or piles of worn-out tires. Or maybe dead batteries!"

But this time, when Agent 1 opened the doors, she was happy to see both a lake AND her friend Miss 2!

"I wonder if Miss 2 knows there is a huge Triple Mouse following her! I'd better go tell her!" And Agent 1 rushed through the old barn doors. Well, as it turns out, Miss 2 had had a cheese sandwich for lunch and the Triple Mouse could still smell it! Doesn't the Triple Mouse look bigger than ever? I wouldn't give him any more cheese to eat!

HANDS-ON:
Write the 4s problems on a whiteboard or scratch paper. Have the child(ren) close their eyes and picture the images that go with each problem. They can draw the big doors and the pictures that were painted on the doors. The answer will be drawn in between the doors. Have them practice retelling the stories.

PRACTICE PROBLEMS:
Use sheets 8.1–8.2 from page 111.

Tactile and kinesthetic activities for learning 4s

FOR ANYONE:

It will be helpful for the student(s) to study the four 4s problems using tactile materials. You can use anything from pebbles to plastic counters for this exercise.

For 4 x 4 = 16, have the child(ren) count out 16 items from their pile.
First they can arrange them into four groups of 4. Ask them what will happen if they combine two of the groups to make an 8 and then do the same with the other two groups. They will now have a combination that is very familiar to them—2 x 8 = 16! It is the picture of two spiders on a 16 spiderweb. Ask them to find out if they can divide the 16 counters into any other equal combination besides the four groups of 4 and the two groups of 8. They may discover that they can make eight groups of 2, and if they do, compare these groups to 2 groups of 8.

For 4 x 6 = 24, have the child(ren) count out 24 items from their pile.
Again, ask the child(ren) to make new combinations with their counters. Of course each pile must be equal to the others. Compare 2 x 12 with 4 x 6. The lesson to be learned in this activity is that you can start with two numbers, and in order to make new combinations, if you double one number, you must halve the other number for the new problem to work out.

For 4 x 7 = 28, have the child(ren) count out 28 items from their pile.
Point out that out of the four problems in this chapter, the 7 is the only odd number. The only other combination that coordinates with this problem is 2 x 14. You halve the first number (4) and double the second (7).

For 4 x 8 = 32, have the child(ren) count out 32 items from their pile.
Have the child(ren) experiment with combinations of numbers. It might seem that many combinations of numbers would be possible, but 2 x 16 and 4 x 8 are actually the only possible combinations.

STORY PROBLEMS:
1- "How would you solve this? Multiplication or division? There were 28 children in 7 rows in the classroom. How many children were in each row?" (Division)

2- "How would you solve this? Multiplication or division? 4 children each planted 8 flowers. How many flowers did they plant in all?" (Multiplication)

PRACTICE PROBLEMS:
Use sheet 8.3 from page 112.

SIX, SIX, PICK UP STICKS

Henormous was looking for more room for her nests. If you remember, each of her nests held six eggs. Well, all her hens kept laying eggs faster than she could make room for them! She felt she really had to find more space. Her chicken house was packed from wall to wall. But first, before we follow Henormous, take a peek at this chart:

Chart for 6x				
6 x 1 = 6	6 x 2 = 12	6 x 3 = 18	6 x 4 = 24	6 x 5 = 30
6 x 6 = 36	**6 x 7 = 42**	**6 x 8 = 48**	6 x 9 = 54	6 x 10 = 60
6 x 11 = 66	6 x 12 = 72			

I colored in the boxes that contain answers we already know. There are only three stories of 6s left to learn!

Anyway, back to Henormous and her search for a new place for her nests! Almost right away, Henormous came upon a darling house with a stick roof. "This would be perfect to hold 6 of my nests," Henormous said. But, unfortunately, there was a huge mouse wearing shades guarding the house. A HUGE Triple Mouse!

"Good morning, Luv," said Henormous in a sweet voice.
"Humph," said the giant Triple Mouse.
So that was that. Henormous went home. (Can you see this picture in your head and tell me about it?)

The next day, however, she renewed her search. This time she had to find room for SEVEN nests! Those eggs were piling up faster and faster!

She came to a lovely wooden house that she greatly admired. Henormous thought it looked a bit small, but was sure if she got closer, she would find the house was really quite roomy. When she stepped closer, however, Henormous bumped her tall head on the overhanging roof. OW. "I guess this is a bit cramped," she said.

Henormous went home to put an ice pack on her head. (While she's doing that, close your eyes and see Henormous bumping her head on the house. How many nests was she trying to accommodate? You can remember this by remembering that in 2 x 7, the 14 house was made of wood just like the seven.)

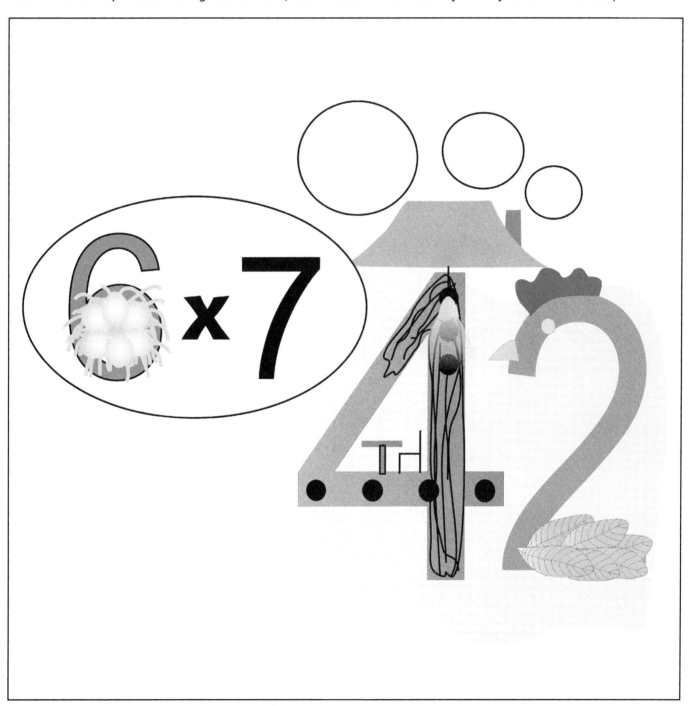

As soon as the bump on her head went down, Henormous set out again. This time she had to find a space that would accommodate EIGHT nests!

Imagine her delight when she came upon another lovely wooden house nestled into the hills by twin lakes. This time when she stepped closer, she didn't bump her head on the overhanging roof. Henormous moved right in! "Just in time for lunch," she said, settling herself at the table. (Again, study this picture and notice that Henormous needed space for 8 nests of 6 eggs. Eight is shaped just like the twin lakes! Can you see all this when you close your eyes and think about the story and the picture you saw?)

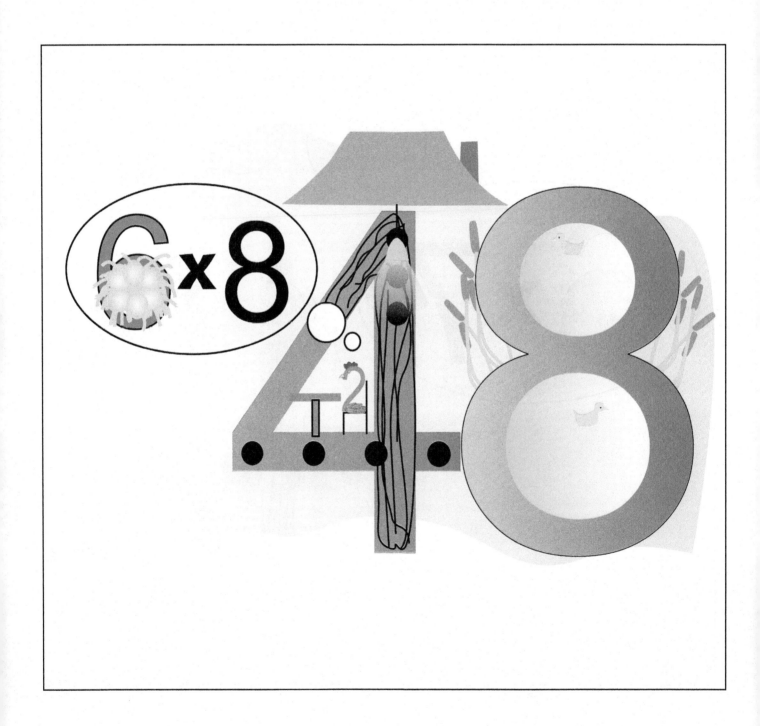

HANDS-ON:
Write the 6s problems on a whiteboard or scratch paper. Have the child(ren) close their eyes and picture the images that go with each problem. Have them draw the images and tell the story.

PRACTICE PROBLEMS:
Use sheets 9.1–9.2 from page 113.

Tactile and kinesthetic activities for learning 6s

FOR ANYONE:

One thing that makes learning 6s simpler is that three of these problems have a bit of a bouncy rhyme to them: 6 x 4 = 24, 6 x 6 = 36, and 6 x 8 = 48. Relate two of these problems to each other, pointing out that 6 x 8 will be exactly twice as large a number as 6 x 4. Ask the child(ren) to make these problems with their real objects so they can see and feel the relationship between the two problems.

Have them play around with other combinations of numbers that make a 24 or a 48.

6 x 7 = 42 and the answer to this problem is the same as 6 x 4 except that the numbers are reversed!

The best reminders for these problems, however, will be the story and visuals.

STORY PROBLEMS:
1- "How would you solve this? Multiplication or division? 48 children went on a field trip. If they were grouped into 8 groups, how many children were in each group?" (Division)

2- "How would you solve this? Multiplication or division? 7 children went hunting for four leaf clovers. If each of them found 6, how many did they find in all?" (Multiplication)

PRACTICE PROBLEMS:
Use sheet 9.3 from page 114.

SEVENS & THE HELIUM BALLOON FAIR

Summer had come with its warm, windy days that made everyone want to be outside enjoying the sun after a long winter. The Sevens decided it would be a super idea to have a balloon fair. What is a balloon fair, you ask? I asked the Sevens the same thing, and frankly I don't think they knew themselves. I think their basic idea was to invite a lot of people to the fairgrounds and then show off a lot of unusual helium balloons and offer them for sale.

Before we head out to the fairgrounds, let's look at the 7s table—I promise it won't take long!

Chart for 7x				
7 x 1 = 7	7 x 2 = 14	7 x 3 = 21	7 x 4 = 28	7 x 5 = 35
7 x 6 = 42	**7 x 7 = 49**	**7 x 8 = 56**	7 x 9 = 63	7 x 10 = 70
7 x 11 = 77	7 x 12 = 84			

Wow! We only have two problems left to look at. Pay close attention to the pictures for these problems.

So off to the fairgrounds we go. Stay with me; this is going to be a quick trip!

At the field, sure enough, we find the Sevens—two of them. But no one has shown up, and we can see why! The wind is blowing up such a gale!

We catch a quick look at the Sevens' balloons— they sure are cool! One is shaped like a puffy 4 and the other like a puffy 9. Together they make a puffy 49. But take a look for yourself. Can't you just feel the wind blowing?

We don't stay at the fairgrounds very long.

We (that's Mr. 5 and I) do come back the next day. You can plainly see the wind has died down. Mr. Seven's hair is all coifed and neat instead of blowing straight back from his face. WOW. We really admire the lovely, brilliant 8-shaped balloon he's got today.

I open my pink purse and buy two matching 8 balloons. One is blown up but the other one isn't.
We look rather nice in this portrait don't we? It will remind us that 56 = 7 x 8. (Notice it is like counting up: 5, 6, 7, 8. So when you see 56 ÷ 7 you will remember the 8 balloon. For 56 ÷ 8 you will remember Mr. 7.)

PRACTICE PROBLEMS:
Use sheets 10.1–10.3 from pages 115–116.
For follow-up, ask the child(ren) if they would like to draw their own pictures for these two problems.

11 EIGHT MAKES HER ESCAPE

Once I got my lovely 8 balloons in my hands, I rushed to the lake.

But I'm getting ahead of myself.

Chart for 8x				
8 x 1 = 8	8 x 2 = 16	8 x 3 = 24	8 x 4 = 32	8 x 5 = 40
8 x 6 = 48	8 x 7 = 56	**8 x 8 = 64**	8 x 9 = 72	8 x 10 = 80
8 x 11 = 88	8 x 12 = 96			

I won't point out we only have one new problem to look at. There it is!

And here I am with my beautiful balloons. I decided to blow up the other 8 balloon so I could really go out in style.

(Notice, will you, that when you say 8 x 8 = 64, you are counting backwards by 2s.)

Well, that is the end of chapter 11.

Why don't you draw your own picture for 8 x 8 = 64 since we finished so quickly? See if you can see it in your head first, though! And you get to decide where I am off to in my boat!

PRACTICE PROBLEMS:
Use sheets 11.1–11.3 from pages 117–118.

90

APPENDIX A

STUDENT PRACTICE SHEETS

1.1 PRACTICE PROBLEMS

$0 \times 5 =$ _____

$71 \times 0 =$ _____

$25 \times 0 =$ _____

$0 \times 867 =$ _____

$124 \times 0 =$ _____

$18 \times 0 =$ _____

$0 \times 42 =$ _____

$12{,}367 \times 0 =$ _____

$58 \times 0 =$ _____

$63 \times 0 =$ _____

$0 \times 352 =$ _____

$4 \times 0 =$ _____

1.2 PRACTICE PROBLEMS

$0 \div 20 =$ _____

$0 \div 4 =$ _____

$0 \div 17 =$ _____

$0 \div 390 =$ _____

$0 \div 2 =$ _____

$0 \div 15 =$ _____

$0 \div 18 =$ _____

$0 \div 8 =$ _____

$0 \div 30 =$ _____

$0 \div 110 =$ _____

$0 \div 29 =$ _____

$0 \div 387 =$ _____

1.3 PRACTICE PROBLEMS

10 x 6 = _____   5 x 10 = _____   10 x 3 = _____

13 x 10 = _____   10 x 2 = _____   9 x 10 = _____

10 x 125 = _____   125 x 10 = _____   10 x 4 = _____

7 x 10 = _____   18 x 10 = _____   10 x 8 = _____

1.4 PRACTICE PROBLEMS

20 ÷ 10 = _____   420 ÷ 10 = _____   50 ÷ 10 = _____

390 ÷ 10 = _____   70 ÷ 10 = _____   630 ÷ 10 = _____

80 ÷ 10 = _____   940 ÷ 10 = _____   30 ÷ 10 = _____

110 ÷ 10 = _____   350 ÷ 10 = _____   60 ÷ 10 = _____

1.5 PRACTICE PROBLEMS

100 x 21 = _____   3 x 100 = _____   100 x 8 = _____

23 x 100 = _____   54 x 100 = _____   100 x 91 = _____

17 x 100 = _____   100 x 43 = _____   100 x 72 = _____

5 x 100 = _____   100 x 65 = _____   7 x 100 = _____

1.6 PRACTICE PROBLEMS

1,200 ÷ 100 = _____   2,100 ÷ 100 = _____   4,500 ÷ 100 = _____

2,300 ÷ 100 = _____   5,600 ÷ 100 = _____   300 ÷ 100 = _____

2,400 ÷ 100 = _____   52,300 ÷ 100 = _____   100 ÷ 100 = _____

900 ÷ 100 = _____   3,600 ÷ 100 = _____   700 ÷ 100 = _____

1.7 PRACTICE PROBLEMS

100 x 21 = _____   2,100 ÷ 100 = _____   3 x 100 = _____

100 x 8 = _____   23 x 100 = _____   52,300 ÷ 100 = _____

54 x 100 = _____   25 x 0 = _____   100 x 91 = _____

4,500 ÷ 100 = _____   0 x 867 = _____   100 x 43 = _____

100 x 72 = _____   2,400 ÷ 100 = _____   5 x 100 = _____

12,367 x 0 = _____   10 x 7 = _____   1,200 ÷ 100 = _____

2,300 ÷ 100 = _____   17 x 100 = _____   100 ÷ 100 = _____

5,600 ÷ 100 = _____   10 x 3 = _____   300 ÷ 100 = _____

2.1 PRACTICE PROBLEMS

$1 \times 56 =$ _____ $98 \times 1 =$ _____ $1 \times 21 =$ _____

$1 \times 3 =$ _____ $76 \times 1 =$ _____ $1 \times 43 =$ _____

$1 \times 99 =$ _____ $12 \times 1 =$ _____ $1 \times 48 =$ _____

$4 \times 1 =$ _____ $27 \times 1 =$ _____ $1 \times 36 =$ _____

2.2 PRACTICE PROBLEMS

$56 \div 1 =$ _____ $21 \div 1 =$ _____ $99 \div 1 =$ _____

$42 \div 1 =$ _____ $16 \div 1 =$ _____ $54 \div 1 =$ _____

$67 \div 1 =$ _____ $81 \div 1 =$ _____ $79 \div 1 =$ _____

$35 \div 1 =$ _____ $94 \div 1 =$ _____ $28 \div 1 =$ _____

2.3 PRACTICE PROBLEMS

5 x 11 = _____   9 x 11 = _____   3 x 11 = _____

6 x 11 = _____   4 x 11 = _____   8 x 11 = _____

7 x 11 = _____   2 x 11 = _____   1 x 11 = _____

2.4 PRACTICE PROBLEMS

22 ÷ 11 = _____   44 ÷ 11 = _____   88 ÷ 11 = _____

66 ÷ 11 = _____   55 ÷ 11 = _____   33 ÷ 11 = _____

11 ÷ 11 = _____   77 ÷ 11 = _____   99 ÷ 11 = _____

2.5 PRACTICE PROBLEMS

11 x 32 = _____   11 x 45 = _____   11 x 81 = _____

11 x 25 = _____   11 x 33 = _____   11 x 63 = _____

11 x 54 = _____   11 x 71 = _____   11 x 90 = _____

11 x 17 = _____   11 x 18 = _____   11 x 72 = _____

11 x 26 = _____   11 x 52 = _____   11 x 62 = _____

2.6 PRACTICE PROBLEMS

11 x 324 = _____   11 x 115 = _____   11 x 621 = _____

11 x 734 = _____   11 x 542 = _____   11 x 5,126 = _____

11 x 345 = _____   11 x 4,243 = _____   11 x 245 = _____

11 x 467 = _____   11 x 683 = _____   11 x 797 = _____

11 x 589 = _____   11 x 367 = _____   11 x 6,543 = _____

Right-Brained Multiplication & Division, © 2011 Sarah Major, Child1st Publications, www.child-1st.com.

2.7 PRACTICE PROBLEMS

$187 \div 11 =$ _____ $154 \div 11 =$ _____ $132 \div 11 =$ _____

$143 \div 11 =$ _____ $198 \div 11 =$ _____ $165 \div 11 =$ _____

$990 \div 11 =$ _____ $781 \div 11 =$ _____ $594 \div 11 =$ _____

$363 \div 11 =$ _____ $275 \div 11 =$ _____ $891 \div 11 =$ _____

$495 \div 11 =$ _____ $352 \div 11 =$ _____ $286 \div 11 =$ _____

2.8 PRACTICE PROBLEMS

11 x 2 = _____   1 x 9 = _____   11 x 9 = _____

99 ÷ 11 = _____   11 x 5 = _____   11 x 8 = _____

11 x 7 = _____   33 ÷ 11 = _____   11 x 32 = _____

11 x 4 = _____   66 ÷ 11 = _____   1 x 21 = _____

88 ÷ 11 = _____   11 x 11 = _____   132 ÷ 11 = _____

11 x 3 = _____   110 ÷ 11 = _____   1 x 16 = _____

11 x 542 = _____   8 x 1 = _____   11 x 115 = _____

11 x 1 = _____   187 ÷ 11 = _____   1 x 27 = _____

3.1 PRACTICE PROBLEMS

$2 \times 9 =$ _____ $2 \times 7 =$ _____ $2 \times 2 =$ _____

$2 \times 5 =$ _____ $2 \times 3 =$ _____ $2 \times 11 =$ _____

$2 \times 4 =$ _____ $2 \times 8 =$ _____ $2 \times 6 =$ _____

$2 \times 10 =$ _____ $2 \times 0 =$ _____ $2 \times 1 =$ _____

3.2 PRACTICE PROBLEMS

$8 \div 2 =$ _____ $10 \div 2 =$ _____ $6 \div 2 =$ _____

$18 \div 2 =$ _____ $12 \div 2 =$ _____ $14 \div 2 =$ _____

$16 \div 2 =$ _____ $22 \div 2 =$ _____ $20 \div 2 =$ _____

$4 \div 2 =$ _____ $2 \div 2 =$ _____ $0 \div 2 =$ _____

3.3 PRACTICE PROBLEMS

$18 \div 2 =$ _____

$2 \times 8 =$ _____

$22 \div 2 =$ _____

$2 \times 1 =$ _____

$6 \div 2 =$ _____

$2 \times 11 =$ _____

$4 \div 2 =$ _____

$2 \times 0 =$ _____

$2 \times 3 =$ _____

$6 \div 2 =$ _____

$2 \times 3 =$ _____

$6 \div 2 =$ _____

$2 \times 9 =$ _____

$14 \div 2 =$ _____

$2 \div 2 =$ _____

$12 \div 2 =$ _____

$2 \times 4 =$ _____

$16 \div 2 =$ _____

$20 \div 2 =$ _____

$2 \times 10 =$ _____

$2 \times 5 =$ _____

$2 \times 2 =$ _____

$10 \div 2 =$ _____

$2 \times 7 =$ _____

Right-Brained Multiplication & Division, © 2011 Sarah Major, Child1st Publications, www.child-1st.com.

4.1 PRACTICE PROBLEMS

12 x 2 = _____   12 x 4 = _____   12 x 3 = _____

12 x 1 = _____   12 x 11 = _____   12 x 6 = _____

12 x 9 = _____   12 x 10 = _____   12 x 5 = _____

12 x 7 = _____   12 x 12 = _____   12 x 8 = _____

4.2 PRACTICE PROBLEMS

48 ÷ 12 = _____   36 ÷ 12 = _____   12 ÷ 12 = _____

24 ÷ 12 = _____   72 ÷ 12 = _____   108 ÷ 12 = _____

84 ÷ 12 = _____   132 ÷ 12 = _____   144 ÷ 12 = _____

60 ÷ 12 = _____   120 ÷ 12 = _____   96 ÷ 12 = _____

4.3 PRACTICE PROBLEMS

12 x 2 = _____

48 ÷ 12 = _____

144 ÷ 12 = _____

72 ÷ 12 = _____

12 x 3 = _____

12 ÷ 12 = _____

60 ÷ 12 = _____

36 ÷ 12 = _____

12 x 11 = _____

36 ÷ 12 = _____

12 x 6 = _____

12 x 10 = _____

12 x 9 = _____

108 ÷ 12 = _____

12 x 5 = _____

12 x 7 = _____

12 x 12 = _____

12 x 8 = _____

24 ÷ 12 = _____

12 x 4 = _____

96 ÷ 12 = _____

84 ÷ 12 = _____

12 x 1 = _____

132 ÷ 12 = _____

Right-Brained Multiplication & Division, © 2011 Sarah Major, Child1st Publications, www.child-1st.com.

5.1 PRACTICE PROBLEMS

3 x 5 = _____   1 x 5 = _____   9 x 5 = _____

2 x 5 = _____   4 x 5 = _____   5 x 5 = _____

8 x 5 = _____   7 x 5 = _____   6 x 5 = _____

12 x 5 = _____   10 x 5 = _____   11 x 5 = _____

5.2 PRACTICE PROBLEMS

15 ÷ 5 = _____   55 ÷ 5 = _____   30 ÷ 5 = _____

45 ÷ 5 = _____   60 ÷ 5 = _____   25 ÷ 5 = _____

10 ÷ 5 = _____   5 ÷ 5 = _____   20 ÷ 5 = _____

35 ÷ 5 = _____   40 ÷ 5 = _____   50 ÷ 5 = _____

5.3 PRACTICE PROBLEMS

$9 \times 5 =$ _____

$50 \div 5 =$ _____

$6 \times 5 =$ _____

$35 \div 5 =$ _____

$40 \div 5 =$ _____

$1 \times 5 =$ _____

$30 \div 5 =$ _____

$55 \div 5 =$ _____

$4 \times 5=$ _____

$7 \times 5 =$ _____

$60 \div 5 =$ _____

$20 \div 5 =$ _____

$3 \times 5 =$ _____

$25 \div 5 =$ _____

$45 \div 5 =$ _____

$2 \times 5 =$ _____

$10 \div 5 =$ _____

$8 \times 5 =$ _____

$5 \times 5 =$ _____

$30 \div 5 =$ _____

$10 \times 5 =$ _____

$11 \times 5 =$ _____

$15 \div 5 =$ _____

$12 \times 5 =$ _____

Right-Brained Multiplication & Division, © 2011 Sarah Major, Child1st Publications, www.child-1st.com.

6.1 PRACTICE PROBLEMS

4 x 9 = _____   2 x 9 = _____   8 x 9 = _____

5 x 9 = _____   7 x 9 = _____   6 x 9 = _____

9 x 9 = _____   3 x 9 = _____   10 x 9 = _____

11 x 9 = _____   12 x 9 = _____   1 x 9 = _____

6.2 PRACTICE PROBLEMS

72 ÷ 9 = _____   18 ÷ 9 = _____   45 ÷ 9 = _____

27 ÷ 9 = _____   54 ÷ 9 = _____   90 ÷ 9 = _____

99 ÷ 9 = _____   81 ÷ 9 = _____   108 ÷ 9 = _____

63 ÷ 9 = _____   36 ÷ 9 = _____   9 ÷ 9 = _____

6.3 PRACTICE PROBLEMS

$2 \times 9 =$ _____ $8 \times 9 =$ _____ $3 \times 9 =$ _____

$72 \div 9 =$ _____ $45 \div 9 =$ _____ $36 \div 9 =$ _____

$5 \times 9 =$ _____ $7 \times 9 =$ _____ $4 \times 9 =$ _____

$90 \div 9 =$ _____ $18 \div 9 =$ _____ $27 \div 9 =$ _____

$6 \times 9 =$ _____ $9 \times 9 =$ _____ $1 \times 9 =$ _____

$54 \div 9 =$ _____ $108 \div 9 =$ _____ $81 \div 9 =$ _____

$9 \times 10 =$ _____ $11 \times 9 =$ _____ $9 \times 12 =$ _____

$63 \div 9 =$ _____ $9 \div 9 =$ _____ $99 \div 9 =$ _____

Right-Brained Multiplication & Division, © 2011 Sarah Major, Child1st Publications, www.child-1st.com.

7.1 PRACTICE PROBLEMS

3 x 4 = _____   3 x 1 = _____   3 x 2 = _____

3 x 8 = _____   3 x 6 = _____   3 x 10 = _____

3 x 7 = _____   3 x 3 = _____   3 x 9 = _____

3 x 12 = _____   3 x 5 = _____   3 x 11 = _____

7.2 PRACTICE PROBLEMS

3 ÷ 3 = _____   12 ÷ 3 = _____   6 ÷ 3 = _____

36 ÷ 3 = _____   27 ÷ 3 = _____   15 ÷ 3 = _____

18 ÷ 3 = _____   9 ÷ 3 = _____   30 ÷ 3 = _____

33 ÷ 3 = _____   21 ÷ 3 = _____   24 ÷ 3 = _____

7.3 PRACTICE PROBLEMS

$36 \div 3 =$ _____ $27 \div 3 =$ _____ $15 \div 3 =$ _____

$3 \times 8 =$ _____ $3 \times 6 =$ _____ $3 \times 10 =$ _____

$33 \div 3 =$ _____ $21 \div 3 =$ _____ $24 \div 3 =$ _____

$3 \times 12 =$ _____ $30 \div 3 =$ _____ $3 \times 5 =$ _____

$18 \div 3 =$ _____ $3 \times 1 =$ _____ $12 \div 3 =$ _____

$3 \times 2 =$ _____ $9 \div 3 =$ _____ $3 \times 3 =$ _____

$6 \div 3 =$ _____ $3 \times 4 =$ _____ $3 \times 9 =$ _____

$3 \times 7 =$ _____ $3 \div 3 =$ _____ $3 \times 12 =$ _____

Right-Brained Multiplication & Division, © 2011 Sarah Major, Child1st Publications, www.child-1st.com.

8.1 PRACTICE PROBLEMS

4 x 5 = _____   4 x 1 = _____   4 x 2 = _____

4 x 8 = _____   4 x 6 = _____   4 x 10 = _____

4 x 7 = _____   4 x 11 = _____   4 x 9 = _____

4 x 12 = _____   4 x 3 = _____   4 x 4 = _____

8.2 PRACTICE PROBLEMS

4 ÷ 4 = _____   12 ÷ 4 = _____   8 ÷ 4 = _____

32 ÷ 4 = _____   24 ÷ 4 = _____   40 ÷ 4 = _____

16 ÷ 4 = _____   36 ÷ 4 = _____   28 ÷ 4 = _____

44 ÷ 4 = _____   20 ÷ 4 = _____   48 ÷ 4 = _____

8.3 PRACTICE PROBLEMS

$16 \div 4 =$ _____

$4 \times 1 =$ _____

$36 \div 4 =$ _____

$28 \div 4 =$ _____

$4 \times 6 =$ _____

$24 \div 4 =$ _____

$4 \times 10 =$ _____

$4 \div 4 =$ _____

$12 \div 4 =$ _____

$8 \div 4 =$ _____

$4 \times 7 =$ _____

$4 \times 9 =$ _____

$32 \div 4 =$ _____

$4 \times 8 =$ _____

$40 \div 4 =$ _____

$4 \times 12 =$ _____

$48 \div 4 =$ _____

$4 \times 3 =$ _____

$4 \times 5 =$ _____

$44 \div 4 =$ _____

$4 \times 4 =$ _____

$20 \div 4 =$ _____

$4 \times 2 =$ _____

$4 \times 11 =$ _____

9.1 PRACTICE PROBLEMS

8 x 6 = _____   9 x 6 = _____   2 x 6 = _____

10 x 6 = _____   7 x 6 = _____   4 x 6 = _____

5 x 6 = _____   1 x 6 = _____   11 x 6 = _____

12 x 6 = _____   3 x 6 = _____   6 x 6 = _____

9.2 PRACTICE PROBLEMS

6 ÷ 6 = _____   24 ÷ 6 = _____   18 ÷ 6 = _____

36 ÷ 6 = _____   12 ÷ 6 = _____   60 ÷ 6 = _____

54 ÷ 6 = _____   42 ÷ 6 = _____   66 ÷ 6 = _____

30 ÷ 6 = _____   48 ÷ 6 = _____   72 ÷ 6 = _____

9.3 PRACTICE PROBLEMS

$48 \div 6 =$ _____ $8 \times 6 =$ _____ $66 \div 6 =$ _____

$2 \times 6 =$ _____ $24 \div 6 =$ _____ $10 \times 6 =$ _____

$7 \times 6 =$ _____ $72 \div 6 =$ _____ $4 \times 6 =$ _____

$30 \div 6 =$ _____ $5 \times 6 =$ _____ $54 \div 6 =$ _____

$11 \times 6 =$ _____ $42 \div 6 =$ _____ $12 \times 6 =$ _____

$3 \times 6 =$ _____ $12 \div 6 =$ _____ $6 \times 6 =$ _____

$6 \div 6 =$ _____ $9 \times 6 =$ _____ $18 \div 6 =$ _____

$36 \div 6 =$ _____ $1 \times 6 =$ _____ $60 \div 6 =$ _____

10.1 PRACTICE PROBLEMS

1 x 7 = _____   11 x 7 = _____   2 x 7 = _____

10 x 7 = _____   4 x 7 = _____   3 x 7 = _____

6 x 7 = _____   7 x 7 = _____   9 x 7 = _____

5 x 7 = _____   12 x 7 = _____   8 x 7 = _____

10.2 PRACTICE PROBLEMS

14 ÷ 7 = _____   70 ÷ 7 = _____   84 ÷ 7 = _____

21 ÷ 7 = _____   63 ÷ 7 = _____   42 ÷ 7 = _____

35 ÷ 7 = _____   28 ÷ 7 = _____   77 ÷ 7 = _____

56 ÷ 7 = _____   7 ÷ 7 = _____   49 ÷ 7 = _____

10.3 PRACTICE PROBLEMS

21 ÷ 7 = _____   10 x 7 = _____   63 ÷ 7 = _____

42 ÷ 7 = _____   1 x 7 = _____   77 ÷ 7 = _____

11 x 7 = _____   2 x 7 = _____   35 ÷ 7 = _____

8 x 7 = _____   28 ÷ 7 = _____   49 ÷ 7 = _____

70 ÷ 7 = _____   12 x 7 = _____   4 x 7 = _____

3 x 7 = _____   56 ÷ 7 = _____   7 ÷ 7 = _____

6 x 7 = _____   14 ÷ 7 = _____   7 x 7 = _____

9 x 7 = _____   84 ÷ 7 = _____   5 x 7 = _____

Right-Brained Multiplication & Division, © 2011 Sarah Major, Child1st Publications, www.child-1st.com.

11.1 PRACTICE PROBLEMS

8 x 8 = _____   8 x 2 = _____   8 x 7 = _____

8 x 11 = _____   8 x 4 = _____   8 x 9 = _____

8 x 6 = _____   8 x 10 = _____   8 x 3 = _____

8 x 1 = _____   8 x 5 = _____   8 x 12 = _____

11.2 PRACTICE PROBLEMS

64 ÷ 8 = _____   80 ÷ 8 = _____   32 ÷ 8 = _____

8 ÷ 8 = _____   24 ÷ 8 = _____   40 ÷ 8 = _____

72 ÷ 8 = _____   16 ÷ 8 = _____   96 ÷ 8 = _____

56 ÷ 8 = _____   48 ÷ 8 = _____   88 ÷ 8 = _____

11.3 PRACTICE PROBLEMS

8 x 8 = _____   16 ÷ 8 = _____   8 x 2 = _____

80 ÷ 8 = _____   8 x 7 = _____   96 ÷ 8 = _____

8 x 11 = _____   24 ÷ 8 = _____   8 x 4 = _____

88 ÷ 8 = _____   8 x 9 = _____   48 ÷ 8 = _____

8 x 6 = _____   40 ÷ 8 = _____   72 ÷ 8 = _____

8 x 10 = _____   32 ÷ 8 = _____   8 x 3 = _____

56 ÷ 8 = _____   8 x 1 = _____   64 ÷ 8 = _____

8 x 5 = _____   8 ÷ 8 = _____   8 x 12 = _____

Right-Brained Multiplication & Division, © 2011 Sarah Major, Child1st Publications, www.child-1st.com.

APPENDIX B

PRACTICE PROBLEM ANSWER KEY

PLEASE NOTE: answers are provided in rows exactly as they appear in the worksheets.

1.1 and 1.2

0 for all problems

1.3

60	50	30
130	20	90
1,250	1,250	40
70	180	80

1.4

2	42	5
39	7	63
8	94	3
11	35	6

1.5

2,100	300	800
2,300	5,400	9,100
1,700	4,300	7,200
500	6,500	700

1.6

12	21	45
23	56	3
24	523	1
9	36	7

1.7

2,100	21	300
800	2,300	523
5,400	0	9,100
45	0	4,300
7,200	24	500
0	70	12
23	1,700	1
56	30	3

2.1

56	98	21
3	76	43
99	12	48
4	27	36

2.2

56	21	99
42	16	54
67	81	79
35	94	28

2.3

55	99	33
66	44	88
77	22	11

2.4

2	4	8
6	5	3
1	7	9

2.5

352	495	891
275	363	693
594	781	990
187	198	792
286	572	682

2.6

3,564	1,265	6,831
8,074	5,962	56,386
3,795	46,673	2,695
5,137	7,513	8,767
6,479	4,037	71,973

2.7

17	14	12
13	18	15
90	71	54
33	25	81
45	32	26

2.8

22	9	99
9	55	88
77	3	352
44	6	21
8	121	12
33	10	16
5,962	8	1,265
11	17	27

3.1

18	14	4
10	6	22
8	16	12
20	0	2

3.2

4	5	3
9	6	7
8	11	10
2	1	0

3.3

9	16	11
2	3	22
2	0	6
3	6	3
18	7	1
6	8	8
10	20	10
4	5	14

4.1

24	48	36
12	132	72
108	120	60
84	144	96

4.2

4	3	1
2	6	9
7	11	12
5	10	8

4.3

24	4	12
6	36	1
5	3	132
3	72	120
108	9	60
84	144	96
2	48	8
7	12	11

5.1

15	5	45
10	20	25
40	35	30
60	50	55

5.2

3	11	6
9	12	5
2	1	4
7	8	10

5.3

45	10	30
7	8	5
6	11	20
35	12	4
15	5	9
10	2	40
25	6	50
55	3	60

6.1

36	18	72
45	63	54
81	27	90
99	108	9

6.2

8	2	5
3	6	10
11	9	12
7	4	1

6.3

18	72	27
8	5	4
45	63	36
10	2	3
54	81	9
6	12	9
90	99	108
7	1	11

7.1

12	3	6
24	18	30
21	9	27
36	15	33

7.2

1	4	2
12	9	5
6	3	10
11	7	8

7.3

12	9	5
24	18	30
11	7	8
36	10	15
6	3	4
6	3	9
2	12	27
21	1	36

8.1

20	4	8
32	24	40
28	44	36
48	12	16

8.2

1	3	2
8	6	10
4	9	7
11	5	12

8.3

4	4	9
7	24	6
40	1	3
2	28	36
8	32	10
48	12	12
20	11	16
5	8	44

9.1

48	54	12
60	42	24
30	6	66
72	18	36

9.2

1	4	3
6	2	10
9	7	11
5	8	12

9.3

8	48	11
12	4	60
42	12	24
5	30	9
66	7	72
18	2	36
1	54	3
6	6	10

10.1

7	77	14
70	28	21
42	49	63
35	84	56

10.2

2	10	12
3	9	6
5	4	11
8	1	7

10.3

3	70	9
6	7	11
77	14	5
56	4	7
10	84	28
21	8	1
42	2	49
63	12	35

11.1

64	16	56
88	32	72
48	80	24
8	40	96

11.2

8	10	4
1	3	5
9	2	12
7	6	11

11.3

64	2	16
10	56	12
88	3	32
11	72	6
48	5	9
80	4	24
7	8	8
40	1	96

CPSIA information can be obtained
at www.ICGtesting.com
Printed in the USA
BVOW11s1245210716

456279BV00011B/102/P